T0243355

PRAISE FOR *HOODWINKED*

"Reverend Amanchukwu is one of those rare Christians who takes the fight to the enemy, instead of just waiting around for someone else to engage. There is a war on our children in America, and as parents, it's our number-one job to protect them. John is leading by example. We need more fighters like him."

—**John Rich**, singer and songwriter

"I highly recommend *Hoodwinked: 10 Lies Americans Believes and the Truth That Will Set Them Free*. Pastor John Amanchukwu's passion for turning people to God as the source of the ultimate truth is contagious. I applaud him not only for this excellent book but also for his work in confronting these lies head on in his travels to school boards across the country."

—**Honorable Bob McEwen**, former U.S. House of Representatives member from Ohio

"I'm thankful Pastor John so skillfully exposes the lies the enemy is trying to get us to believe. Every Christian needs to have his new book. We all need to make sure our pastors read this and get on board—we need to ensure no one gets *Hoodwinked* ever again!"

—**Victor Marx**, high-risk humanitarian and founder of All Things Possible Ministries, VictorMarx.com

"John Amanchukwu is a voice of strength, integrity, faith, and boldness that this generation desperately needs. I'm proud to be his pastor, mentor, and father-in-law. I'm blessed to see the impact of his work in my time."

—**Bishop Patrick L. Wooden Sr.**, Upper Room Church of God in Christ

"In *Hoodwinked*, Pastor John Amanchukwu boldly tells the truth about ten of the most divisive issues in our country today with the same courage and conviction he brings to truth-telling at a school board meeting, in his church, and everywhere he preaches. Patriots everywhere need to rally around this message and this man."

—**Sebastian Gorka, Ph.D.,** host of "America First" podcast and former deputy assistant to the president

HOOD
WINKED

JOHN K. AMANCHUKWU SR.

HOOD WINKED

10 LIES AMERICANS BELIEVE AND THE TRUTH THAT WILL SET THEM FREE

REGNERY
FAITH

Published in the United States by Regnery Faith, an imprint of Skyhorse Publishing, Inc.

Regnery® is a registered trademark and its colophon is a trademark of Skyhorse Publishing, Inc. a Delaware corporation.

10 9 8 7 6 5 4 3 2

Library of Congress Cataloging-in-Publication Data is available on file.

Print ISBN: 978-1-68451-692-6
eBook ISBN: 978-1-5107-8150-4

Cover design by CU Creative Co.
Cover photograph by Davonte Anthony

Printed in the United States of America

This book is dedicated to TEAM Amanchukwu, the fruit and posterity of the Wooden, Weeks, and McNeil families.

To my loving, caring, strong, fervent, virtuous, and bonny wife, Crystal, I salute you for your unfailing support and diligence in being the consummate homemaker while working outside of the home. You are to be commended, revered, and honored, for you're irreplaceable in our family. May we grow old together and drive slow upon busy roads in the distant future. My love for you endures a lifetime.

To John Patrick, my oldest child, who made me a proud father first; to Pamelyn Jewel, who will be Daddy's princess forever, and to John Jr., aka "Spiderman," keep webbing the villains of this age and foes to come—may the words and truth that emanate from these pages be a guidepost for the legacy of the Amanchukwu family.

Your name has great meaning: Amanchukwu means "I know God," and it's my prayer and commitment that you serve the God of the Bible for all your days.

CONTENTS

CONTENTS

FOREWORD

Two and a half centuries ago, America's Founders established their new nation upon self-evident truths: That all men are created equal, and that they possess the inalienable rights to life, liberty, and pursuit of happiness.

But that was 250 years ago. Today, America is not a republic of self-evident truths, but under the regime of self-evident lies. These lies claim that America is a racist country, that only future discrimination can fix past discrimination, and that our well-being today requires killing off our future. Those spreading these lies claim that if we just spend enough time pumping poison into children's brains at a young age, it will remove "stigma" and those poisons will cease to be poisonous.

Nobody understands the threats we live under better than my good friend Pastor John K. Amanchukwu. He and I both know what it's like to be pilloried and denounced for preaching the Gospel. John has been called a "book burner" for trying to make sure kids learn math and reading in school instead of being given pornography. He's been called a race traitor for trying to save unborn black lives.

Pastor John breaks the mold in another way: He is as bold as a lion in a time when most pastors are cowards. The past few years have sometimes been heartbreaking for me. I've seen pastors shy away from crucial moral questions like sexual purity, the sanctity of marriage, or the right to life, because they think speaking about the core moral issues of the present is too "political" for Christian leaders. I had to watch thousands of pastors call themselves "non-essential" and gladly close their churches to worshipers for weeks or even months at a time. I've seen pastors who fear their neighbors more than they fear God, and who fear dying most of all—and why would anyone want to follow a "Christian" who is worried about dying?

John, on the other hand, fears only God, and whether he's taking on school boards or abortionists, he never wilts under pressure, intimidation, or social scorn. He knows that any pastor worth his salt must be a true leader in the community, not just a life coach who is heard on Sundays and otherwise forgotten. He knows that preaching the Gospel should be risky—just as it was risky for Christ two thousand years ago.

Yet for all his bravery, John has always been one of the most personable and humane pastors I know, and I am glad to count him as a friend as well as an inspiration.

Read this book, take it in, and then put it into practice in your own life. Learn how to tear down the façade of lies that dominates our country, and rebuild the deeply moral, Christian nation that this land is supposed to be. You won't regret it.

Charlie Kirk
Founder, Turning Point USA

INTRODUCTION

THE LIES THAT MAKE US

If a ruler listens to lies, all his officials become wicked.
—Proverbs 29:12

We live in an age of misinformation. Just scroll through your favorite social media app, and you'll be confronted by fact-checkers and flags designed to highlight information on posts that is deemed to be spurious at best. Helpful, right? Except that more often than I can count, the "misinformation" turned out to be true, and the official story trumpeted by government authorities and parroted by the mainstream media turned out to be false.

As I write this, news outlets all over the world are talking about a hospital in Gaza that was bombed by the Israeli Defense Forces in the war against the Palestinian terror organization Hamas. Five hundred innocent civilians were killed, they tell us. The print edition of the *New York Times* on October 18, 2023, even showed an above-the-fold image of the hospital's smoking remains. But there was a problem with this narrative: It came from Hamas, and the *Times* didn't even question it. The truth is, a Hamas rocket from inside Gaza misfired, landing in the hospital parking lot.[1]

But the *Times* didn't stop with sloppy reporting. It went even further by falsifying the photographic evidence: The image was of another hospital from an unrelated incident.[2]

The *New York Times* was once "the paper of record," but now it's as unreliable as Sunday morning gossip at church. Even worse, it's all too often caught pushing a radical leftist agenda that has no basis in the truth. (The Sunday morning gossips at least start with some small kernel of fact.) So much for objective journalism.

Whether you're talking about COVID-19 treatments, the outcome of the 2020 election, the truth about Hunter Biden's laptop, or the dangers of a high-fat diet, you can find answers from across the political spectrum. Many people will say they're busting through the "misinformation shield" that's been keeping the truth about what's going on in the world from the American public. A few years ago, if you believed in UFOs, you would have been considered slightly to the left of crazy, but now, even the U.S. government says they are, in fact, real.[3] Turns out they just have been lying to us for decades. The so-called fact-checkers are supposed to protect us from these things, but their corrections often come too late or not at all when there's an agenda to push. And this method of hiring "neutral" people to fact-check everything—including our opinions—seems a poor substitute for free speech.

The problem is, lies are not harmless. They hurt people because they color reality. Repeat a lie long enough, and it becomes accepted as truth, despite evidence to the contrary. Tell me again how Joe Biden received eighty-one million votes in 2020. Sure. All those votes that came in the middle of the night while the voting tabulation machines were down and then "found" after they came back online were all *definitely* on the up-and-up. It's just a coincidence that anyone in the public eye who questioned the official narrative was silenced, canceled, or otherwise destroyed. And talk about a lie that has hurt our country! Stolen elections have consequences, as we all now can see plainly for ourselves.

This book in your hands is about some of the lies that harm our country and our world. They're not of the UFO or Hunter's laptop variety; they're bigger than those. These are the persistent lies that undermine who we are as a people and affect our future. They're the kind of lies that few dare challenge because they are repeated so often and questioning these narratives might make a person unpopular in certain circles. Truth be told, there are more lies than these harming our society (so don't be surprised if one day you see a book with the subtitle *10 More Lies Americans Believe*). But as a husband and father, pastor, and black American who loves Jesus, these are the lies that are most personal to me—so this is where I've chosen to begin.

Lies are funny things. To wield them to full effect, they have to contain a spark of truth—or at least enough plausibility to make us question the truth. When the serpent slithered up to Eve in the Garden of Eden, it wasn't with a whopper that would be revealed as obviously false in the light of Paradise. Rather, it was with a subtle twist on the truth:

> Now the serpent was more crafty than any of the wild animals the LORD God had made. He said to the woman, "Did God really say, 'You must not eat from any tree in the garden'?"
>
> The woman said to the serpent, "We may eat fruit from the trees in the garden, but God did say, 'You must not eat fruit from the tree that is in the middle of the garden, and you must not touch it, or you will die.'"

"You will not certainly die," the serpent said to the woman. "For God knows that when you eat from it your eyes will be opened, and you will be like God, knowing good and evil." (Genesis 3:1–5)

Satan's desire was to get the humans to doubt God's goodness, to believe their Creator was holding out on them. Humanity was made in God's image (Genesis 1:26–27). They were already like God in every way that matters because He had designed them that way—to be His human family. On the surface, it would seem, then, that Satan's temptation should have fallen flat. After all, at that moment, Eve was standing in a beautiful paradise with everything she could ever need or want. But notice what Satan added: "You will be like God, *knowing good and evil*" (3:5, emphasis added).

Our first parents knew what "good" was. They were surrounded by it. They lived in it. They were the product of it. But evil was foreign to them. Satan's choice of words made it seem plausible that perhaps God was indeed holding out on them. And the devil wasn't entirely lying, either. The moment Adam and Eve ate from the forbidden fruit of the Tree of the Knowledge of Good and Evil, "the eyes of both of them were opened" (v. 7). They did indeed come to know evil, but not in the sense of being wise about it; rather, they were thrust into it. They knew it experientially. The world around them changed. Sin entered in and brought Death with him. Suffering, pain, and sickness would now be a part of life on Earth. Adam and Eve knew good and evil, all right.

Every lie we'll discuss in this book is like that. This is one of the reasons they're so powerful. But that's all the more reason we need to confront them and learn the real truth. Nothing shatters darkness like a strong beam of light, and nothing kills a lie faster than a strong dose of truth.

Over the past couple of years, I've earned a nickname: The Book-Banning Pastor. That's because I've frequently attended local school board meetings to read from the filthy books those boards, teachers, and librarians are foisting upon our children. (See chapter 8 for more on those adventures.) I don't perform stunts to grab attention, and I don't lecture the ne'er-do-wells across from me with biblical ethics; I simply read the trash they believe is appropriate for kids to ingest. And guess what? They always stop me. They shout over me. They turn off my mic. (Good thing I have a booming preacher's voice!) They escort me out of the building. They've been hoodwinked into believing that these disgusting, pornographic books are good and appropriate for kids. But in fact, these books have always been part of an agenda to groom kids into sexual perversion. I stand up and reveal truth.

I tell you this to let you know I'm in the truth-revealing business. I guess that's part of being a pastor. But it's also part of being a Christian, and it used to be part of being an American. So, I've written this book to arm you in the culture war. This is a war not against flesh and blood, but against ideas. As Paul writes in Ephesians 6:12, "Our struggle is not against flesh and blood, but against the rulers, against the authorities, against the powers of this dark world and against the spiritual forces of evil in the heavenly realms." Make no mistake: there is demonic power behind many of the lies ensnaring our culture. That is why cold facts alone will not save the day. We need spiritual truth, Gospel power, and prayer.

As you come to this book, you may be a believer. Or you may not be. The fact that you picked up this book in the first place tells me you're concerned about the direction of our nation— and that you have a thirst for truth. Please know that no matter what your background may be or where you currently stand on the lies presented in this book, you are welcome here. One of the problems in our current cultural moment is that we're very quick to shut others up when we disagree. We translate our personal offenses into a right not to be offended that we have made up ourselves. (See chapter 6 on that whopper.) But that is one of the ways lies spread.

While I hope this book is informative, and even entertaining in places, I also hope it will be one of the ways God arms you for the fight in which we find ourselves. Every chapter counters a particularly egregious lie with real-world data. In addition, Scripture is included throughout so that you might know these rebuttals are not merely the opinions of a so-called troublemaking preacher. They are based in the Word of God.

During His earthly ministry, Jesus said, "If you hold to my teaching, you are really my disciples. Then you will know the truth, and the truth will set you free" (John 8:31–32). Today, there are plenty of people who claim to be Jesus's followers. But, as He said, a person is only His disciple if they follow His teachings. His teachings—as well as His life, death, and resurrection—are the truth we desperately need.

As a nation, we've drifted far from the Judeo-Christian ethics that once filled our public square. I believe America will be saved, but it won't be without a struggle. Every person who loves God and wants to see His will accomplished on this planet needs to hold on to the truth like never before. It is the only way we will ever find our freedom again. It is the only way America will once more live up to the promise of being the land of the free and the home of the brave.

For too long, we have allowed the lies of progressives and race-baiters to go unanswered. Christian believers and conservatives alike tend to go about life with a live-and-let-live attitude. But in doing so, we have allowed our culture's most powerful institutions to become indoctrination centers for each succeeding generation. Our universities, K–12 public school system, Silicon Valley, Hollywood, the mainstream media, and Wall Street are in lockstep with cultural Marxists who don't want anyone to be truly free. And yet, we have something they don't have: the truth. No matter what they try to tell us, a man cannot become a woman, America is not a racist nation, and porn is not reading material for kids. So, as Paul instructed believers nearly two thousand years ago: "Stand your ground" (Ephesians 6:13).

☞

THE TERM *"HOODWINKED"* is antiquated, no doubt. But it perfectly describes the danger of the lies we face in our nation today. The word originally described a person who had a hood pulled over their head so that they were beyond blindfolded. There was no peeking out of the corners of the fabric or squirming to see shapes in the distance. If a hood were pulled over your head, you would be blind, helpless to see your true situation. And it wouldn't matter how much light were to shine on your face, because it wouldn't get through the hood.

The problem with being blind is that blind people don't know what they're missing. Jesus said as much when He described a group of Pharisees who were teaching the people doctrines of men that were opposed to the heart of God: "Leave them; they are blind guides. If the blind lead the blind, both will fall into a pit" (Matthew 15:14). I firmly believe there are good people in this country. Many of them wholeheartedly disagree with me on some of the core issues we'll talk about in the following pages—but that's only because they have been walking through this world with hoods pulled over their heads. Years of indoctrination, easy answers, and being shouted at by those who control the microphone have left them unable to realize that they've been deceived.

It's not enough to speak truth; we must also dismantle the lies. May this simple book remove some hoods.

John K. Amanchukwu Sr.
October 19, 2023

CHAPTER 1

LIE #1: AMERICA IS A RACIST NATION

*I will permit no man to narrow and degrade
my soul by making me hate him.*
—Booker T. Washington

I t's a bold statement, one as wide as the miles between Portland, Oregon, and Portland, Maine, and as dark as the bloodstained sin of slavery. To say that the United States of America is a racist nation, a country that is irredeemably prejudiced against its own black citizens, is no small thing. Such a notion can't simply be taken at face value. It requires examination and reflection, and even soul-searching.

There are many who want us to believe racism in America is as obvious as gravity, as self-evident as the truths our nation's allegedly racist Founders wrote about in the Declaration of Independence. The country's bigotry runs so deep, they tell us, that the only remedy is to burn down its institutions and start over. These ideas are now widespread, filling our social media feeds and occupying much of the twenty-four-hour cable news cycle. Our schools have even been infiltrated by the ideas presented in the 1619 Project, and so our youngest and most innocent citizens have learned to parrot adults' talking points about America's alleged systemic racism.

Every time an act that could be construed as racist takes place somewhere within our shores, the mainstream media and politicians in Washington point and scream, "See! This country is racist!" That tactic is used frequently because it is effective. In April 2023, 59 percent of those surveyed by NBC News said American society is racist.[1]

But isolated incidents overflowing from ugly hearts do not characterize the masses. The nature of a nation's soul cannot be determined by its worst examples or an opinion poll.

It's easy to focus on the negative stories. When a young man like Ahmaud Arbery is murdered while jogging in a mostly white neighborhood because his dark skin makes it appear to his killers that he must be a criminal,[2] it's right to take notice and speak up. It's right to cry, to be outraged, to demand justice. But I am convinced that for every hate crime committed against black people in this country, there are many more acts of kindness going unreported. Love rarely makes the evening news. It seldom goes viral.

In my own life, I have received tremendous blessings from my white brothers and sisters. In fact, it's fair to say I wouldn't be where I am today without the generosity of people that I'm told, every day, must be secretly racist.

☞

As I WALKED up to the front doors of Cardinal Gibbons High School, I'm not sure what I was expecting to happen. It was a private school, and my family didn't have private-school money. My mom was already performing an impossible feat by feeding and clothing four children on $28,000 a year; there was simply no way she could afford to pay that kind of tuition. And yet, the doors of that private Catholic high school were opened to me.

Bishop Michael Burbidge, who oversaw North Carolina's Diocese of Raleigh—and Cardinal Gibbons High School—had implemented a policy: The school would never turn away any student for financial reasons. And so, for my junior and senior years, I received a full scholarship.

But that wasn't all: Every month, Brother Gary, one of the school's administrators, would call me into his office, pull out his old brown-leather wallet, pull out five crisp twenty-dollar bills, and hand them to me. "Go, eat," he'd say. He knew my family didn't have much money, and he wanted to make sure I didn't have to go without.

I'd always smile and shake Brother Gary's hand. I didn't know how to thank him, but I appreciated his kindness deeply. The first time that happened, I was in shock. The next month, when he did it again, I couldn't believe it. After a few more months, I assumed he would eventually stop. But he never did. Every month that I was a student at Cardinal Gibbons, Brother Gary gave me a hundred dollars of spending money just to bless me. And that wasn't all, either! Every year when the fair came to town, he would give me three hundred dollars and tell me to share it with my siblings. At Thanksgiving and again at Christmas, he would send me home with a big basket of food as well.

Not once did Brother Gary hand me a gift in public; it was always behind closed doors, away from the other students. He practiced Jesus's teaching when He said, "But when you give to the needy, do not let your left hand know what your right hand is doing, so that your giving may be in secret" (Matthew 6:3–4). It wasn't common knowledge that I was on a full, need-based scholarship, either. I wasn't treated any differently from anyone else; I was a member of the student body, at home at Cardinal Gibbons. Brother Gary and the other faculty at the school provided for my financial needs, but they also protected my dignity along the way.

There are millions of people like Brother Gary across this land—men and women who are generous and caring, and who don't discriminate based on the color of someone's skin. They see the humanity of every person they meet. They don't always do the right thing, but when they realize they've made a mistake, they try to do better. Kindness is hard to forget, so I think about my years at Cardinal Gibbons a lot these days. I think about Brother Gary and the way I felt the first time he handed me a hundred dollars, no strings attached.

So many voices are telling us America is a racist nation. It's repeated ad nauseam—so often, in fact, that many people assume it must be true. In a study conducted in 2019, 84 percent of black respondents said discrimination was a major obstacle for them, while only 54 percent of white respondents thought discrimination was a problem for black people. Similarly, 83 percent of black respondents said they thought they were generally treated unfairly by the police, while only 63 percent of white respondents believed black people had a tougher time with law enforcement.[3]

At first glance, it may appear these numbers simply reflect lived experiences. For some respondents, that may be the case. However, political affiliation also revealed a vast disparity in the same survey: 84 percent of Democrats said racist and racially insensitive viewpoints have become more common, and 64 percent said such opinions are also more acceptable in our society. Meanwhile, only 42 percent of Republicans said racist attitudes have become more common, and just 22 percent said they were more accept-able now than in years past.[4]

Some people will look at these statistics and say to them-selves, *Well, that proves it! America really is a racist country! After all, why would so many people attest to seeing something that isn't there?* But there's a big difference between people believing America itself must be racist and many people in America actually being racist.

If America were truly a racist nation—one that hated people with brown skin—why would brown- and black-skinned immigrants be flocking to our borders, as they cur-rently are? According to the Pew Research Center, as of 2019, one in ten black Americans—about 4.6 million people—were immigrants, meaning they were born in another coun-try. By 2060, that number is expected to more than double to 9.5 million.[5] If America were really a racist place, why would the highest median income belong to Asians, rather than white people?[6] If America were just brimming with white supremacists, bigots, and racist hatemongers, how in the world did the nation elect a black president in 2008? And then reelect him in 2012?

☞

Is AMERICA RACIST? It's an important question and one we should not wave away lightly. At the same time, I think it might actually be the wrong question to ask. You see, racism is a part of our history, and its effects are still being felt. The chattel slavery of Africans for nearly 250 years is not easily wiped away. Segregation and Jim Crow laws, redlining and unequal protection under the law—these things are racist and ugly, and without a doubt, they have left their scars on generations of black Americans. In this sense, yes, America has been stained by the sin of racism. There can be no doubt about it. But that doesn't mean the United States has always been uniformly racist or that things haven't improved significantly over time.

Over the course of American history, slavery has been a divisive issue. It was never unanimously celebrated or condoned. There have always been men and women—black and white—who have stood up to oppose the practice.

At our nation's founding, the issue was so explosive it nearly upended negotiations among the thirteen colonies. Many of the men who gathered in Philadelphia for the Second Continental Congress wanted slavery abolished in an independent America. Thomas Jefferson, who's often touted as a wicked slaveholder by the Left, actually drafted a section of the Declaration of Independence condemning the slave trade, calling it "execrable commerce" and an "assemblage of horrors."[7] The passage was removed to appease slaveholding state representatives in the hopes of creating a final document everyone would willingly sign. However, within the Declaration's wording about "all men" being "created equal," Jefferson and others planted the seeds for the eventual abolition of slavery.

More than four score, that is, eighty, years later, Abraham Lincoln recognized the genius of our country's Founders and saw in the opening lines of the Declaration of Independence the truth that would set the captive African slaves free:

This was their majestic interpretation of the economy of the Universe. This was their lofty, and wise, and noble understanding of the justice of the Creator to His creatures. Yes, gentlemen, to *all* His creatures, to the whole great family of man. In their enlightened belief, nothing stamped with the Divine image and likeness was sent into the world to be trodden on, and degraded, and imbruted by its fellows.

They grasped not only the whole race of man then living, but they reached forward and seized upon the farthest posterity. They erected a beacon to guide their children, and their children's children, and the countless myriads who should inhabit the earth in other ages.

Wise statesmen as they were, they knew the tendency of prosperity to breed tyrants, and so they established these great self-evident truths, that when in the distant future some man, some faction, some interest, should set up the doctrine that none but rich men, or none but white men, were entitled to life, liberty, and pursuit of happiness, their posterity might look up again to the Declaration of Independence and take courage to renew the battle which their fathers began—so that truth, and justice, and mercy, and all the humane and Christian virtues might not be extinguished from the land; so that no man would hereafter dare to limit and circumscribe the great principles on which the temple of liberty was being built.[8]

The pro-slavery movement was never monolithic; there were always critics, detractors, and revolutionaries willing to fight to bring freedom to every American. Speaking of the fight for freedom, let's never forget the price that was paid to set black slaves free. Approximately 360,000 Union soldiers gave their lives to end slavery and reunite our severed country,[9] and when you add in all those who were wounded, captured, or missing in action, the number balloons to nearly 600,000.[10] A racist country doesn't send its young men to die to set black slaves free.

When it comes to the Jim Crow era of America's story, the situation is similar. Very often, white business owners in the South are presented as stone-cold racists who wanted nothing more than to keep blacks away from their lunch counters and out of their "whites only" restrooms. However, it's important to remember that Jim Crow was never optional. It was the law of the land, handed down from the state legislatures, which were, in large measure, controlled by Democrats. It was a crime to violate the racist codes. Business owners were not free to disregard the statutes without consequence. Does that excuse segregation? Of course not. Does it mean there weren't many business owners who were, in fact, racist? Certainly, the answer is no. But it does mean that, once again, painting with a broad brush seems to distort the picture rather than preserve it.

In nearly every area that can be measured, the circumstances of black Americans have improved over time. In 1964, just 27 percent of black Americans over the age of twenty-five had a high school diploma, but by 2015 that number had risen to 88 percent.[11] College graduate rates have also increased. In 1980, only 10.5 percent of black people in the United States had completed college,[12] but today 45.9 percent have a college degree.[13] When it comes to income, there is still a considerable disparity between white and black households, but the wealth of black Americans continues to rise:

> The Black middle-class has also grown substantially since 1967. Using the three middle income groups from Census ($35,000 to $100,000), it has more than doubled in absolute terms from 2 million to well over 4 million. It has shrunk slightly as a proportion of the total, but of course for good reason: more Black families are above $100,000. If you prefer to change the definition of middle class slightly, say to the range of $50,000–$150,000, it looks even better: it grew from 1.3 million in 1967 to 4.5 million in 2021, more than tripling! And by this second definition, it grew in percentage terms too (28% to 44%).[14]

It's worth asking: Would a racist country really allow black Americans to achieve the American dream? As Dennis Prager has suggested, "The left-wing charge that America is a racist country is the greatest national libel since the Blood Libel against the Jews. America is, in fact, the least racist multiracial, multiethnic country in world history."[15]

I UNDERSTAND A bit about upward mobility. When I was a child, my mother moved our family to Raleigh, North Carolina, where, for several months, we lived in a homeless shelter. After that, we moved to the projects. And from there we moved into a Habitat for Humanity house. My mom was able to improve our situation through hard work and a little something called never giving up—and she was sustained by her faith in Jesus. Sometimes she worked as many as sixteen hours a day to make sure we had a roof over our heads and food in our bellies. Because of my mom's diligence, my siblings and I developed a strong work ethic. Today, we are all comfortably middle class, and our families are thriving.

Of course, there are many black Americans today who believe the lie that America is racist, and that it's this racism that has kept them from success. It's not just black Americans who believe this, either; there are plenty of people from every race perpetuating this dangerous propaganda. It's easy to see why the Left pushes the race card every day of the year. They might as well shout, "America is broken, and the deck is stacked against you! You'll never succeed on your own! But if you vote for us, we'll give you everything you need!" Incidentally, this is also the reason the media depicts the GOP as a party that's intrinsically racist—never mind the fact that it was the Republican Party that ended slavery and its members who voted in higher percentages than Democrats for the Civil Rights Act of 1964.

The Democrat Party uses (and abuses) their black voters. But why—oh, why?—do people fall for it? If Democrat policies actually improved the lives of black Americans and other minority groups, our nation's Democrat-run cities would be bastions of opportunity and prosperity. But of course they're not. There were 774 murders in Chicago in 2020.[16] Of those, 95 percent of the victims were people of color![17] And if statistics hold true, 70 percent of the people who murdered them were also people of color.[18]

The notion that America is a racist nation is not just a lie; it's also a temptation. Think about it for a moment: If the education system is out to see you fail, and the banking system is out to keep you poor, and the real estate market means to keep you in the projects, then your life is not your responsibility. In other words, if America is hopelessly racist, anyone who's not white is a victim—and in our society today, victimhood has tremendous power.

Being a victim is a mindset, a way of thinking that affects every part of life. If we accept the false premise that America hates brown and black people, then we fall into the trap of victimhood, and everything in our world can be viewed only through that lens. It's a truly diabolical trap.

But there is hope. There is a way to remove the shackles of victimhood and counter the lies being shot at us rapid-fire from leftists seeking to unravel the very fabric of our society. The lie of America's persistent and unbridled racism may have the power to transform free people into victims—most lies from the pit of Hell are quite potent, after all—but the truth is more powerful still. The truth has the power to set captives free, to change the world and bring light to the darkness.

No matter how hard the race-baiters and pot-stirrers may try, they cannot change the nature of things. They cannot transform a person's identity, and they cannot bring peace through the division and chaos they sow. The most they can do is blind people, at least temporarily. But God's Word declares the truth from beginning to end. It has not been changed to fit a political agenda, and it stands as an invitation to walk a better path, to know the living God and His Son, Jesus Christ.

The Bible declares that all people were created as God's image-bearers. Therefore, every single human being has value—black and white and every shade of melanin in between. God loved us so much that while we were slaves to our sins, caught in open rebellion against our Maker, Jesus died for us. He did this to bring us home to God, that we might live out our intended design as His sons and daughters. Those of us who know Christ have been adopted into royalty, given a priesthood, and commissioned as ambassadors of Heaven. If we know this—and I mean really know it, deep down in the depths of our being—it affects how we live out our days in this fallen world.

A child of the King cannot be a slave or a victim. Not really, anyway. Any suffering or injustice they experience in this world will be swallowed up by Christ's victory. They have hope beyond what they can see with their eyes. Caleb and Joshua knew this. If you recall, these two men were among the twelve Israelite spies sent to investigate the land of Canaan, the land God had promised to His people (see Numbers 13). While the other ten spies returned quaking in fear and defeat, complaining about the giants of the land, Caleb and Joshua saw the opportunity through the lens of God's goodness to their people and declared their trust in His promises. They held tightly to the truth of God's word, pushing aside every lie of the enemy—even when those lies seemed to be true. Decades later, the other ten spies were dead and buried; only Caleb and Joshua entered the land of promise.

But many Christians have not learned how to walk in faith; they don't know what it is to keep their eyes fixed upon Jesus. That is why the Bible tells us, "Do not conform to the pattern of this world, but be transformed by the renewing of your mind" (Romans 12:2). The battle is not really *out there*. It's not against another race or a political party or even a system that may discriminate against us. The real battle is in the mind, so it is essential that we fill our minds with the truth. If we do, there's no lie big enough to take us down.

This can be seen throughout American history. Consider the life of Booker T. Washington, for example. He was born a slave and lived through some of the most difficult years of racism and prejudice our country has ever known. But he refused to give up and consign himself to a life of destitution. Washington was industrious and never backed down from a challenge. It was his Christian faith that kept him going, and he died a very wealthy man. Against all odds, he made his own success because he believed what God said about him, not what other people wanted him to believe.

In 1895, Washington delivered a speech at the Atlanta Exposition. He declared that African Americans should focus on vocational education. Learning Latin and Greek served no purpose in the day-to-day realities of Southern life.

African Americans should abandon their short-term hopes of social and political equality. Washington argued that when whites saw African Americans contributing as productive members of society, equality would naturally follow.

For those dreaming of a black utopia of freedom, Washington declared, "Cast down your bucket where you are." Many whites approved of this moderate stance, while African Americans were split. Critics called his speech the Atlanta Compromise and accused Washington of coddling Southern racism.

Still, by 1900, Washington was seen as the leader of the African American community. In 1901, he published his autobiography, *Up from Slavery*. He was a self-made man and a role model to thousands. In 1906, he was summoned to the White House by President Theodore Roosevelt. This marked the first time in American history that an African American leader received such a prestigious invitation.[19]

Washington's life created no small measure of controversy. By refusing to stand up against every racial injustice black Americans in the South faced in his day, some believed he was merely an apologist for the white majority. But I don't see things quite that way. Yes, I believe strongly we should stand up against any and all bigotry. However, Washington understood the best way to elevate the status of his brothers and sisters throughout the South was not to fight a second Civil War—one they would likely lose—but to encourage and inspire people of color to make the most of their lives with the resources at their disposal—and those resources certainly included the good gifts the Lord had given them. He also understood that even though America was not a perfect nation, it provided opportunities other lands did not. And so, he allowed his gratitude and his self-determination to chart his course. You be the judge: Did it work out well for him?

I imagine that if Washington could have looked down the corridors of history to our day, tears would well up in his eyes for all that black Americans have accomplished. There's still more room to grow, of course. But the path forward is not paved with discontent; it is built on the optimism that can come only when we believe what God has declared about our worth, not what the denizens of dark corners of humanity have said about us.

☞

THERE'S A STORY my wife, Crystal, tells about a home she never lived in. In the 1980s, when Crystal was a young girl, her father wanted to buy a new house for their family in a beautiful little neighborhood in Rockingham, North Carolina. He made an appointment with a real estate agent to look at homes in that subdivision, but the agent kept trying to steer him away from that particular neighborhood. No matter what he said, she would insist on looking at other properties.

Crystal's father decided that if the agent wouldn't take him to look at those houses, he would go on his own. So, one day he drove out to the neighborhood to look around. Within a few minutes, he was greeted by another agent who worked for the homebuilder. She was even more gruff than the first agent! It was then that he got the message: his black family was not welcome in that neighborhood.

One day, years later, when the family was driving through that part of Rockingham, Crystal's dad pointed out the subdivision and told about his experience there years earlier. But rather than being angry, he was smiling as he reminisced. Why? Because he realized that God had blessed him in such a way that he could now buy all the homes in that little subdivision if he wanted to.

There are—and always have been—bigots in this country. But the story of America is the story of a people trying to live up to the ideal that "all men are created equal." This isn't a perfect place, but it is a good place filled with good people. And thanks be to God, it is still a land of opportunity for men and women of every color.

CHAPTER 2

LIE #2: BEING PRO-LIFE IS ONLY FOR WHITE EVANGELICALS

Human beings cannot give or create life by themselves;
it is really a gift from God. Therefore, one does not
have the right to take away (through abortion)
that which he does not have the ability to give.
—Jesse Jackson

There were eighty-five of us outside—men and women, black and white—joined together in common cause. We were there as Christians who believe abortion is the murder of unborn children. Our protest was not the marching-with-signs-and-shouting-demands sort. We prayed, we spoke to people coming and going, and we made our presence known. There was no violence, of course—at least not there on the sidewalk. The only violence that day was kept in the back rooms where tiny, still-forming boys and girls were being mutilated in the most unjust of executions.

The sign on the building—A Woman's Choice—demanded to have the final word on the matter, but we knew the ending of a baby's life should not come down to mere "choice." Everyone, no matter how small or how vulnerable, has a right to life. So we lifted our voices to Heaven, appealing to God to intervene, to change hearts and minds so that these little ones might survive the day.

I'm a big guy—a former collegiate football player and all—so I'm not accustomed to being confronted aggressively in public. That's why I was surprised when the door to the clinic burst open and an irate man came out, headed straight toward me. He got in my face, angry as could be. I'd never met this man before, but he had something he wanted to say to me—not to the others in the crowd, but to me alone. It all happened so quickly that it took a few moments for me to process what was happening, but when I did, it all became clear.

"Why are you with them?" he said, gesturing toward the white folks in our group. "Being pro-life is a white man's issue. Don't you know you're black?"

I think about that moment a lot. Thankfully, there was no physical altercation. I spoke to the man calmly but firmly, and after a minute or so, he went back inside to wait for his girlfriend as she endured the abortion that ended the life of their unborn child.

As an outspoken pro-life advocate, I hear this sort of thing all too often. And in one sense, it's true: the pro-life movement has, in large measure, been championed by white Christians, while their black brothers and sisters have been either silent or even vocally pro-abortion. But there's a wide chasm between recognizing the current situation and affirming that the pro-life stance belongs solely to white evangelicals.

☞

THERE ARE PEOPLE who will tell you the Bible does not speak to the issue of abortion. They'll say you can read the book from cover to cover and never even find the word "abortion" in it. Of course, that's true. The term itself is modern, as are the diabolical procedures that are used. But that doesn't mean God's Word is silent on the subject. Several scriptures talk about the sin of murder and the necessity of caring for those who cannot care for themselves, but perhaps my favorite passage on the subject is Proverbs 6:16–19, which says:

> There are six things the Lord hates,
> seven that are detestable to him:
> haughty eyes, a lying tongue,
> a heart that devises wicked schemes,
> feet that are quick to rush into evil,
> a false witness who pours out lies
> and a person who stirs up conflict in the community.

It's right there in the Bible—the same Bible that both black Christians and white Christians read—clear as day: God hates "hands that shed innocent blood" (v. 17). No one is more innocent than an unborn child, no one less able to fend off an attacker than a baby in the womb. And so, rightly, many Christians have read these words and concluded that abortion is an offense against a holy God, a stain on our society, an unspeakable evil that should be abolished.

Why is it, then, that many black Christians today miss this truth? Why are they at odds with white believers when it comes to abortion? Surely, following the written Word of God on a matter as straightforward as this one should unite us, not divide us.

According to the research, the difference may have little to do with faith and almost everything to do with politics. With each election cycle that comes around these days, the vast majority of black voters cast their ballots for the Democratic Party—before the 2022 midterm elections, 70 percent said they planned to vote for Democrat candidates in the House races.[1] According to the pollsters at Gallup, this identification with the DNC is driving black attitudes on abortion:

> This shift in Black Americans' attitudes has not occurred in a vacuum and appears to be closely tied to increasing political polarization on abortion. Party identification is a core demographic variable of interest in today's social, political and cultural environment. Since over three-quarters of Black Americans identify with or lean toward the Democratic Party, any broad trends that differentially affect Democrats' attitudes about abortion are—everything else being equal—going to affect Black Americans' as well.[2]

Over the last couple of decades, there has been a shift in the way black Americans view the issue of abortion. Between 2001 and 2007, 31 percent of them saw abortion as a morally acceptable option. By 2017, that number had jumped to 46 percent.[3] As the culture becomes more divided, views on issues like abortion are being defined by tribe and political party. In other words, as most black Americans have become more entrenched in the Democrat party, the party's values have affected how they understand a basic moral issue like abortion.

A hundred years ago, most black Americans were Republican. After all, the Grand Old Party was the party of Lincoln, the party of emancipation. The first black representatives in Congress were all Republicans.[4] But then something happened during the Great Depression:

Franklin Roosevelt's second administration—led by the New Deal—made the Democrats a beacon for black Americans deeply affected by the crushing poverty that was plaguing the country.[5]

As many as two-thirds of the black population in the United States began voting Democrat. That seems like a high number, but when you realize that, today, about 90 percent of black Americans are committed to the Democratic ticket, it was a relatively low tide. It also wasn't monolithic. In the years that followed the New Deal, many black Americans could still be persuaded to vote for a Republican candidate. At least, that was the case until the 1960s.

In the summer of 1964, Barry Goldwater won the Republican nomination, surprising many pundits. One of his campaign promises had been to let states decide issues like civil rights, though he had conceded that if the Civil Rights Act of 1964 passed, his administration would abide by it. Just two weeks before the Republican National Convention in San Francisco, where Goldwater clinched the nomination, the Civil Rights Act was signed into law. But it didn't matter that he'd promised to respect the decision: His stance on small government communicated a strong message to black voters that the Republican Party had turned its back on them.

President Lyndon B. Johnson, upon signing the bill into law, allegedly said, "I'll have those niggers voting Democratic for the next two hundred years."[6] The vulgar label notwithstanding, he was right. We're now sixty years removed from his words, and black support for the Democrat Party is still holding strong—and with it, tacit support for abortion.

☞

EVEN THOUGH BLACK support for the Democrat Party became nearly universal in the 1960s, support for abortion on demand was not automatic. In fact, many black Christians would attempt to hold the two ideas in tension, calling themselves pro-life Democrats. Even the Reverend Jesse Jackson—the founder of the Rainbow PUSH Coalition, known today for his unwavering support of leftist issues that openly defy the clear teaching of the Bible—was once an outspoken pro-life advocate.

In the March 1973 issue of *Jet* magazine, released just weeks after the unconstitutional *Roe v. Wade* Supreme Court ruling came down, Jackson was quoted as saying,

> Abortion is genocide. Anything growing is living. . . . If you got the thrill to set the baby in motion and you don't have the will to protect it, you're dishonest. . . . You try to avoid reproducing sickness. You try to avoid reproducing deformities. But you don't try to stop reproducing and procreating human life at its best. For who knows the cure for cancer won't come out of some mind of some black child?[7]

This statement makes it clear that Jackson not only saw abortion as an evil practice, but also saw its particularly devastating effects on communities of color across America. In the years that followed, Jackson continued to speak out against abortion. In 1975, he even publicly joined Ruth Bell Graham, the wife of evangelist Billy Graham, in supporting a constitutional amendment to ban abortion in the United States.[8]

In 1977, Jackson spoke at the March for Life rally, and later that year wrote an essay for *National Right to Life News*. In that piece, he identified himself as someone who would likely have been aborted had *Roe v. Wade* been the law of the land when he was growing in his mother's womb. He wrote,

In the abortion debate, one of the crucial questions is when does life begin. Anything growing is living. Therefore human life begins when the sperm and egg join . . . and the pulsation of life takes place. From that point, life may be described differently (as an egg, embryo, fetus, baby, child, teen-ager, adult), but the essence is the same.[9]

It's hard to imagine this Jesse Jackson is the same person who, in the 1980s, began saying "Women must have freedom of choice over what to do over [sic] their bodies."[10]

So what happened? In 1984, the Reverend Jesse Jackson ran for president as a Democrat, and his position on the issue of abortion began to crumble. When asked whether the federal government should provide funding for abortion, he responded, "I would never encourage abortion, except under medically extenuating circumstances. On the other hand I do support freedom of choice."[11] Here, you can see his inconsistency—the personal pro-life stance in opposition to his political pro-choice position.

By 1988, when Jackson ran for president a second time, he had made a complete 180-degree turn from his 1970s pro-life conviction, stating, "It is not right to impose private, religious and moral positions on public policy."[12] This directly contradicts what he had said about the privacy argument more than a decade before:

> If one accepts the position that life is private, and therefore you have the right to do with it as you please, one must also accept the conclusion of that logic. That was the premise of slavery. You could not protest the existence or treatment of slaves on the plantation because that was private and therefore outside your right to be concerned.[13]

Jesse Jackson's evolution on the issue of abortion is tell-ing, and not merely because he's a public figure who's been involved in politics. Are we even surprised anymore when a candidate flip-flops on a controversial topic to woo donors and appease powerful party insiders? That said, Jackson makes an interesting test case. Here is a Baptist minister who once locked arms with conservatives to stand against the clear evils of abortion. But after rising in the Democratic Party, he aban-doned every biblical conviction related to the protection of the unborn. It's not that he doesn't know better—his early analy-sis and commentary tell us that he does. Rather, it's that Jesse Jackson learned to put party above God's commandments.

Sadly, I don't think Jackson is alone. He might have had a brighter spotlight aimed at him than most, but he landed in the same place most black Americans have. Their allegiance to the Democratic Party has shaped their understanding of right and wrong, even to the point where they have allowed being a Democrat to be part of what it means to be a black American. Perhaps that's why there wasn't much of a fuss when, on the campaign trail in 2020, Joe Biden had the audac-ity to say, "If you have a problem figuring out whether you're for me or Trump, then you ain't black."[14] It's as though, with those words, he was simply confirming what LBJ was getting at decades earlier: the Democrat Party owns black voters.

Of course, that's not really true. Every American citizen—black, white, brown, and all shades in between—has the right to vote for any candidate they choose. We are all free to think for ourselves and support whichever party most closely aligns with our values. It's a lie to say that the pro-life cause is a white evan-gelical issue. It's a justice issue, a moral issue, and a sin issue, but it doesn't belong to any one race or voter demographic.

THAT DAY OUTSIDE the abortion clinic, that angry boyfriend got in my face to tell me I was a traitor to our race for praying against the murder to which he was a party. I doubt he realized it, but in that moment, he was being about as racist as anyone can be without putting a bedsheet over their head and carrying a tiki torch. What he was really saying to me was this: "You're black like me. You don't get to have an opinion anymore. You don't get to have convictions. You need to fall in line and do whatever the Democratic Party tells you. They own you, just like they own me!"

Abortion affects communities of color to a greater degree than other communities. That's because Planned Parenthood and other abortion providers strategically place their facilities in black and Hispanic neighborhoods.[15] It's a slow-burning genocide that's celebrated by the very families it seeks to destroy. So, no, the pro-life cause isn't a white evangelical issue. It's an issue for every Christian and everyone who values life. But it ought to be an issue of particular concern to black Americans, especially those who call Jesus their Lord and Savior.

Every child murdered in the womb, burned by chemicals, or torn apart by surgical instruments is a human being who was knit together in the image of God. Each discarded boy or girl, whether tossed in the trash or having his or her organs harvested for sale on the black market, was a vessel of nearly unlimited potential. Every abortion is an unspeakable tragedy, a wrong that can never truly be undone. As Jesse Jackson once said, "For who knows the cure for cancer won't come out of some mind of some black child?" Or some white child. Again, race doesn't matter when it comes to abortion. Every child is precious, and every last one bleeds red.

CHAPTER 3

LIE #3: CAPITALISM IS TO BLAME FOR POVERTY

*Underlying most arguments against the free
market is a lack of belief in freedom itself.*
—Milton Friedman

In a homeless shelter, there are sights and sounds that cling to you. But the thing I remember the most from that season of my life is the fear, the insecurity that overtakes you while you're lying in bed at night trying to fall asleep. By the time you arrive at the shelter, there is nothing left to catch you if you fall. It's the bottom rung of the ladder, a step above living in a car or out on the streets, exposed to the elements. It's a roof above your head, a bed to sleep in, and food to eat. It's a place to survive but not to thrive. No one is there because they want to be.

I was just a kid at the time, but I knew that things weren't supposed to be the way they were for us. My mom had done the best she could, but my dad was out of the picture by that point, and Mom had just a hundred dollars to her name. With four kids to feed, she had no choice but to take us to the shelter. And we were there nearly a year as Mom tried to get her feet underneath her.

There are people who would be ashamed of such a humble valley in their upbringing. But not me. I'm proud of my mom and everything she did for my siblings and me. She worked hard to provide for us, and little by little, she did. Taking us to that shelter was just one of the difficult things she needed to do to make sure we were safe.

Contrary to what you might hear from politicians, we are not a nation composed of static socioeconomic classes. My own life proves that. Many of us will be poor for a season and then rise up into the middle class or even higher. Others will go in the opposite direction. And some will go back and forth more than once. There are many reasons why a person's financial status might change, and this chapter is too short to delve into all the complexities of our modern economy. But it's worth taking the time to debunk one particularly stubborn myth—namely that capitalism is to blame for poverty in the United States.

Jesus famously said, "The poor you will always have with you" (Matthew 26:11). And while He didn't mean that statement as a challenge, it appears that some have taken it as such. No matter what people in power do to alleviate the problem of poverty, they keep proving Jesus right. In fact, many of the government's best intentions over the years have only worsened the plight of the poor. Still, no matter how poverty persists, some will always claim to have the solution. Today, that "solution" is often to get rid of capitalism.

Capitalism, the engine of growth that brings some high, must inevitably bring others low—or at least that's the talking point. But is capitalism really a zero-sum game? Do some people have to lose so others can win? Does the existence of multibillionaires like Elon Musk and Jeff Bezos mean there *necessarily must be* families living in a shelter somewhere?

☞

IT'S HARD TO deny that, on the whole, capitalism has been a force for good in the world. In 1820, when capitalism was not yet widespread, 90 percent of the world lived in poverty. That's hard to believe because our world is so different today. But two hundred years ago, nine out of every ten people in the world were utterly poor. Today, the poverty level is about 10 percent, due in no small part to capitalism's hold on much of the West and its influence in the East.[1]

> Fernand Braudel, the famous French historian, wrote a definitive work on the social history of the 15th to 18th centuries. People's diets, he revealed, largely consisted of porridge, soup and bread made from low-quality flour, which was baked in batches every couple of months and was often moldy and so hard that it could only be cut with an axe. Most people, even in cities, had to get by on 2,000 calories a day, with carbohydrates making up well over 60 percent of the total. Food was often nothing more than a lifetime of eating bread and bread again, or mush and porridge. People back then were lean and small in stature—throughout history, the human body has adapted to inadequate caloric intake.[2]

You might be saying, "Yes, perhaps. But things improved over time because of advancements in technology and new farming techniques. The fact that wealth is widespread today doesn't prove capitalism is the key." But a closer look actually does show a correlation between the introduction of free-market principles and increased Gross Domestic Product (GDP) per capita:

In the first year of our common era, GDP per capita in Western Europe was 576 international dollars, compared to 467 international dollars for the world as a whole. That means that in Europe, GDP per capita doubled in the pre-capitalist period, between year 1 and the year 1820. In the much shorter period from 1820 to 2003, GDP per capita in Western Europe then rose from 1,202 to 19,912 international dollars and in the other capitalist countries of the West it climbed as high as 23,710 international dollars.

But the same progress was not replicated everywhere. In Asia, for example, in the 153 years from 1820 to 1973 GDP per capita only increased from 691 to 1,718 international dollars. And then, in just thirty years, from 1973 to 2003, it rose from 1,718 to 4,344 international dollars.[3]

Today, even in communist China, capitalism is busy boosting the living standards of the people. While the Chinese Communist Party is still a repressive, authoritarian regime with an iron grip on nearly every facet of life, the introduction of certain free-market principles following the death of Mao Zedong in 1976 ushered in a new age of expansion for the traditionally poor nation.[4] It's difficult to imagine any other factor at work in the People's Republic of China that could have produced the same dramatic turnaround.

"Still," people often say, "capitalism favors the rich." Certainly, the wealthy are better off under capitalism than under other economic systems, and oftentimes their wealth grows at a faster rate thanks to the intricacies of compound interest, but it's not only the rich who benefit from the free market. While the rich certainly get richer, so do the poor. Based on the standard of living of the poor in 1980, the consumption poverty rate[5] fell from 13 percent in 1980 to 2.8 percent in 2018.[6] In addition, the life of a poor person today is much different than it was decades ago. As historian Lee Edwards notes, "The reality is that the average 'poor' American owns a car, enjoys air conditioning, has access to the Internet, and has at least one TV. The official poverty line for a family of four is $25,465."[7]

Of course, if you're living on the streets, it doesn't matter if you're a citizen of the freest society in the world. You aren't thinking about GDP per capita if you go to sleep hungry every night. To paraphrase a quotation dubiously (and frequently) attributed to Winston Churchill, "Capitalism is the worst economic system there is—except for all the others." Capitalism is not a perfect system, no matter what some might say. But it is a good system, and it has alleviated poverty for billions of people.

As I write this chapter, the number one song on the Billboard Hot 100 songs chart is "Rich Men North of Richmond" by Oliver Anthony Music, the stage name of Christopher Anthony Lunsford. The lyrics lament the state of the world—how inflation and taxes have ruined a working man's dollar, how politicians and corporate barons have manipulated the system so that, no matter how hard many of us try, we simply can't get ahead. The song wasn't written in some Third World country run by a two-bit dictator, nor was it penned by someone living in communist China. Chris Lunsford lives in Virginia, and when he wrote the powerful tune, capitalism hadn't been much of a friend to him.[8]

Now, I'm not suggesting that Lunsford is bemoaning capitalism in his song. But I bring up "Rich Men North of

Richmond" because it points to the reality that capitalism can be corrupted, and as a result, hard-working people can be left behind. Capitalism is not the easy fix to all the world's economic problems. The last thing I want to suggest is that if you're struggling financially, it's all your fault. Economics is a complicated issue with tons of variables. Someone can do all "the right things" and still end up on the bottom of the socioeconomic ladder.

Even so, true capitalism does two things very well. First, it rewards hard work. Generally speaking, the more someone has to offer, the better their reward. Sometimes it's physical labor or know-how that demands a wage, but other times it's a financial investment, honed talent, a brilliant idea, or a new innovation tested through years of trial and error. Compare that to socialism, where benefits are distributed equally regardless of personal input.

The second thing capitalism does very well is acknowledge the reality of human selfishness. It is the only economic system that does not assume everyone will behave in the best interest of others. Rather, it assumes (rightly) that people naturally act in their own self-interest. But that's not necessarily a bad thing. In a free market, with certain rules in place, everyone doing what's best for their own family will yield wonderful results.

In a famous example, immortalized by Leonard E. Read, a simple pencil is held up as a miracle of capitalism. Without any central planning or committee meetings, thousands of people worked together to create a pencil. Just consider what is involved in merely the first stage of the pencil's "life," logging the cedar:

> My family tree begins with what in fact is a tree, a cedar
> of straight grain that grows in Northern California and

Oregon. Now contemplate all the saws and trucks and rope and the countless other gear used in harvesting and carting the cedar logs to the railroad siding. Think of all the persons and the numberless skills that went into their fabrication: the mining of ore, the making of steel and its refinement into saws, axes, motors; the growing of hemp and bringing it through all the stages to heavy and strong rope; the logging camps with their beds and mess halls, the cookery and the raising of all the foods. Why, untold thousands of persons had a hand in every cup of coffee the loggers drink![9]

Extrapolate this "family tree" out to every stage of a pencil's manufacture, and then trace a similar lineage for every other product available in a free market, and you'll have a basic idea of the power of capitalism and how it has harnessed the human proclivity for self-interest to benefit the world. Once again, the pencil shares its wisdom:

The lesson I have to teach is this: Leave all creative energies uninhibited. Merely organize society to act in harmony with this lesson. Let society's legal apparatus remove all obstacles the best it can. Permit these creative know-hows freely to flow. Have faith that free men and women will respond to the Invisible Hand.[10] This faith will be confirmed. I, Pencil, seemingly simple though I am, offer the miracle of my creation as testimony that this is a practical faith, as practical as the sun, the rain, a cedar tree, the good earth.[11]

GIVEN CAPITALISM'S ABILITY to lift people out of poverty, it shouldn't surprise us that it is rooted in biblical theology.

That's not to say that the Bible prescribes capitalism as the official economic system of the Kingdom of God. Rather, it promotes a certain lifestyle that fundamentally agrees with God's instructions for humanity.

Most importantly, capitalism honors work. Without work, the engine of economic freedom grinds to a halt. Yet many people mistakenly believe that work is a bad thing, that it's a result of the Fall detailed in Genesis 3. But in reality, God designed human beings to work. Eden wasn't a never-ending vacation land where Adam and Eve lounged around the pool and ate bonbons. Scripture says, "The LORD God took the man and put him in the Garden of Eden to work it and take care of it" (Genesis 2:15). That was Adam's purpose: "to work" the garden "and take care of it."

While it's true that the curse of sin made work more difficult, it did not change the fact that work is still part of the "very good" world God created (see Genesis 1:31). We were designed to work. By our very nature, we are meant to be productive and innovative. Any economic system that does not enable human beings to work in freedom stands opposed to the created order.

The Bible places such an emphasis on work that the Apostle Paul instructed believers in Thessalonica, "The one who is unwilling to work shall not eat" (2 Thessalonians 3:10). But in socialism—or even in corrupt, big-government capitalism—people who refuse to work are often rewarded with a check in the mail every month. Of course, there are people who, due to illness or disability, cannot work. Paul was not talking about them, nor does the Bible condemn such people. It's the *unwillingness* to work that God's Word holds up as sinful.

In another place, Paul wrote, "Anyone who does not provide for their relatives, and especially for their own household, has denied the faith and is worse than an unbeliever" (1 Timothy 5:8). We don't just have a responsibility to provide for ourselves through our labor; we must also provide for our immediate family and have something to give should our extended family fall into trouble. By generating an income, we show our love to those closest to us. Elsewhere, the Bible also instructs us to give to the poor and needy (Proverbs 19:17; Luke 6:38)—an income comes in handy there too!

And then there is this famous passage from Proverbs that demonstrates the virtue of work using an illustration from nature:

> Go to the ant, you sluggard; consider its ways and be wise! It has no commander, no overseer or ruler, yet it stores its provisions in summer and gathers its food at harvest.
>
> How long will you lie there, you sluggard? When will you get up from your sleep? A little sleep, a little slumber, a little folding of the hands to rest—and poverty will come on you like a thief and scarcity like an armed man. (Proverbs 6:6–11)

The ant knows the only way to survive is to work. God has given it enough sense to gather more than enough food to eat in season so that it can store additional provisions for the winter. And yet many people lack this same good sense. In our sin, we crave comfort and pleasure. Hard work is, well, hard, while idleness is easy.

☞

AGAIN, CAPITALISM ISN'T a perfect system. There are plenty of people who work very hard and still struggle financially. So please do not think I'm saying that if you're having trouble making ends meet, you must be lazy. I am definitely not saying that. However, in general, capitalism rewards those who take risks and plan ahead. Those who refuse to work are inevitably left behind. And here's the incredible thing about hard work and entrepreneurship: everyone benefits, not just the one who reaps the immediate reward.

Think about Elon Musk for a moment. Right now, as I write this, he's the wealthiest person on the planet. Critics of capitalism would tell you that he has too much money—more than he deserves and more than he could need in a few hundred lifetimes. Under socialism, he'd be forced to give the state most of his earnings in order to provide benefits for everyone else. But would that really be a good thing?

Musk's ingenuity and entrepreneurship have given us services like PayPal, a tool millions of people use every day to make online payments. Through Tesla, he has helped to make electric cars an increasingly viable option for personal and commercial transportation. His Starlink satellites are currently providing high-speed internet service to people in diverse places around the world, all without earthbound infrastructure. SpaceX is allowing NASA to continue space exploration with the goal of eventually landing a human being on Mars. In addition, Musk's Boring Company is developing underground tunnels to ease traffic in large cities. Those are just a few of the high-profile ventures Elon Musk has undertaken—and in the process, he's created thousands upon thousands of jobs, generating wealth for families and communities across the nation. So, the question we must ask is this: Would Musk's profits be better spent by the government or by his own reinvestment? Which would benefit society more in the long run?

Socialism says wealth is the problem. Capitalism says idleness is. Socialism wants central planning and authoritarian control so that no one will step out of line. On the other hand, capitalism only works well if people have a generous measure of economic freedom. Socialism promises that everyone will be treated the same, no matter what each one contributes to society, while capitalism rewards people based on hard work, ingenuity, and the risks they're willing to take. Under socialism, the government picks winners and losers. Under capitalism, individual consumers vote with their dollars, rewarding the best ideas, products, and services, virtually ensuring that innovation will continue.

When you look around and notice that not everything in capitalist America works the way I've described, a light bulb should turn on. As our government grows larger and interferes with more aspects of life every day, the free market we once enjoyed is being increasingly manipulated. Overregulation is stifling competition—to the bliss of large, established corporations, which now don't have to worry about startups stealing their thunder. At the same time, lobbyists and wealthy donors are currying favor with our representatives to make sure laws and tax codes favor their industries, in many cases silencing the power of the consumer. The effect of this "crony capitalism" is that many people are getting the short end of the stick. Many of the rewards of the market are being gamed, not earned. That's not good for anyone, and it breeds cynicism, undermining the very values that would ordinarily promote prosperity.

Even so, the answer is not less capitalism but more. If we hope to help people in poverty—nay, if we truly love our neighbor—one of the most practical things we can do is support policies and candidates that favor free-market economics. More important than that, however, is to develop a mindset that doesn't see hard work as a problem but an opportunity.

☞

THERE IS A tendency to relegate the topic of economics to the lesser, earthly realm of ideas. After all, money is hardly spiritual. It's only good down here, and no one can take it with them when they die. Jesus talked about storing up treasure in Heaven (Matthew 6:20), but not the filthy kind of lucre we have down here.

Even so, anyone who's ever been without it knows money isn't an entirely bad thing. I remember lying awake at night in the shelter, never really being able to rest. No matter how long you stay at a place, if you live in insecurity, it's not really a home. And when you stop to think about it, home really is one of the greatest blessings of capitalism. Only in a free market with private property rights can people build a lasting home.

I am grateful that, today, my three children can go to bed without worrying if they'll have food in the morning. They can sleep soundly, without any fear that their home will be taken from them or that they won't have a bed to sleep in the following night. They are secure in part because capitalism has allowed our family to build wealth and own a piece of the American dream.

Thinking about my kids, I find it interesting that when the prophet Micah described the coming Kingdom of God, he said, "Everyone will sit under their own vine and under their own fig tree, and no one will make them afraid, for the LORD Almighty has spoken" (Micah 4:4). Apparently, private property rights will not be obliterated when Jesus returns in His glory. And that sense of security my children have—the one that I lost for a time when I lived in that shelter? Apparently, that's what God wants for all His children.

CHAPTER 4

LIE #4: CHRISTIANITY IS A WHITE MAN'S RELIGION

*Christianity is not a white man's religion—and don't
let anybody ever tell you that it's white or black. Christ
belongs to all people. He belongs to the whole world.*
—Billy Graham

In the fall of 2022, shortly after the trailer for Disney's live-action remake of *The Little Mermaid* was released online, the hashtag #notmyariel began trending on Twitter (now X). On YouTube, the clip racked up more than a million dislikes in a matter of hours. It was immediately apparent that many viewers were unhappy with one of the studio's casting decisions. Halle Bailey, a rising young black actress, deservedly snagged the lead role, but many Disney fans were not accustomed to seeing Ariel with such dark skin.

In the 1989 animated version of the fairytale, the character had white skin and long, red hair and was voiced by Jodi

Benson, a white actress. Mainstream media outlets were quick to denounce the blowback against Bailey being cast as Ariel as pure racism. Here's how *Rolling Stone* covered it:

> The whiny tweets (which, it should be noted, happen pretty much every time a person of color is cast in a franchise) carried more than a whiff of absurdity, with its implicit suggestion that there's some sort of sanctity involved in the casting of a busty teenage mezzo soprano fish with no legs. Some, however, tried to make the "argument" that because *The Little Mermaid* is based on a Danish fairy tale—specifically, Hans Christian Andersen's *Little Mermaid*—to not cast a Danish-looking (i.e., white) woman would represent a deviation from the source material. Of course, the original version of the story involves Ariel cutting out her tongue in exchange for feet that bleed constantly when she's on land, and ends with her dissolving into sea foam after she considers stabbing Prince Eric and his new wife to death; in the Andersen story, she also has green skin. So by arguing for the need for historical accuracy—again, we're talking about a story about a *mermaid who is best friends with a talking flounder*—racists are once again showing their whole asses.[1]

Though Walt Disney Studios claims its casting decisions had nothing to do with reaching a diversity quota or trying to make a political point,[2] it's understandable that, given our cultural moment, many Disney fans didn't buy it. Some even noted that if the reverse were to happen—if a traditionally black character were to be portrayed by a white actor—it would be decried as black erasure or cultural appropriation and would not be tolerated by progressives or the mainstream media.[3]

Despite the controversy, young girls of color all around the world were elated to see Bailey in the role. Bailey herself said it was those ecstatic responses that got her through all the negativity: "Seeing all the babies' reactions, all the brown and Black young girls, really tore me up emotionally."[4] As it turns out, representation does matter.

Right now, you might be asking yourself what Disney princesses and Twitter trolls have to do with Christianity supposedly being a white man's religion. While many complained that a black Ariel couldn't be "historically accurate" (because all the *real* mermaids we know about from historical records were white, *obviously*) or that Ariel's extra melanin wouldn't do justice to the source material (a Danish fairytale that is likely an allegory about unrequited homosexual advances[5]), these same people don't bat an eye when they see Jesus depicted as a European with fair skin, dirty blonde hair, and piercing blue eyes. It is those images, among other things we'll discuss in this chapter, that have led some people to believe the lie that Christianity belongs exclusively to white people. Worse than that, many believe the religion cannot be used as anything but a cudgel of colonialism, oppression, and racism.

I remember seeing those whitewashed images of Jesus in my Catholic high school. Of course, none of my white classmates or teachers ever said they thought Jesus was actually a white guy. As far as I know, everyone affirmed He was Jewish, of Middle Eastern stock, and likely had brown skin. But the stylized pictures of white Jesus didn't seem to bother anyone in my majority-white high school, either. Although I knew Jesus wasn't European, I couldn't wrap my mind around the pale version of Him staring back at me from within those frames. I knew it wasn't okay for one race to appropriate the Savior like that, no matter how traditional it had become.

NOT LONG AGO, I was a guest on former NBA star Kwame Brown's podcast.[6] He graciously invited me on to talk about my work with school boards in various counties nationwide. You see, when school districts decide that pornographic reading material is suitable for children, I show up at their meetings to let my voice be heard. Many times, I'll read selections from these filthy books, and more often than not, they'll cut off my mic or have security usher me away from the podium. The board members want this overtly sexual and exploitative garbage available in school libraries for kids to read, but for some reason they don't want it read aloud for the public to hear. Strange, right?

Anyway, on Brown's show, I was part of a panel discussion about race in America. One of the panelists—a certain woman who seemed particularly angry—made a remark about immigrants from Africa coming to the United States and adopting white culture. That caught my ear, and I had to ask her about it. I wanted her to define "white culture" for me. I wanted her to explain what made something "white."

At first, she talked in circles, telling me white culture is European culture. Again, I asked, "What does that mean?" I wanted her to be specific, to identify the markings of white culture that should be off-limits to black immigrants. It took a while, but eventually she talked about white Jesus. She told me about a painting of white Jesus her mother had displayed in her home while she was growing up. Apparently, it had made quite an impression—one she still couldn't shake all these years later.

"We know Jesus wasn't white. We know He was Jewish," I told her. Bad art shouldn't get to reject the Gospel. "If He were white, magenta, purple, blue, or canary yellow, I would serve Him," I continued. "But He was Jewish. It wasn't His skin tone that saved me; it was His blood." In that moment, it felt like I was standing up at a school board meeting. I was stating the obvious, but she just wanted to shut me up.

She then told me the real Jews in the Bible were as black as her and that the people who claim to be Jewish today are really only Jewish by religious choice; they aren't the true descendants of Israel. We both tried to keep the conversation civil, but I knew in that moment we were never going to see eye to eye. She was utterly swimming in black liberation theology, and she couldn't get her head above water long enough to see that she was pushing aside true Christianity—trusting Jesus on His own terms—in favor of a false gospel that makes the Christian faith synonymous with being black.

According to black liberation theology, the story of Israel is really the story of oppressed Africans. When Jesus said, "Take up your cross," He meant we should embrace our blackness and follow Him into the ghetto. Black liberation theology focuses on race rather than grace. As one of its main tenets, it declares the inherent righteousness of blackness and the inherent wickedness of whiteness. Thus, God is, in a sense, black. What's more—He is concerned with the salvation of the oppressed but not the repentance of the oppressor. In other words, the Gospel is not for everyone. And in black liberation theology, the great problem of humanity is oppression, not sin. Therefore, sin is redefined so that liberation by any means necessary becomes righteous and good—even if it means using violence.[7] All kinds of evil can be justified if it's perpetrated by black hands against white people. In short, black liberation theology is another gospel, and that means it leads to death.

James Cone, often credited as the pioneer and progenitor of black liberation theology, wrote this about God and blackness:

Because blacks have come to know themselves as *black*, and because that blackness is the cause of their own love of themselves and hatred of whiteness, the blackness of God is the key to our knowledge of God. The blackness of God, and everything implied by it in a racist society, is the heart of the black theology doctrine of God. There is no place in black theology for a colorless God in a society where human beings suffer precisely because of their color. The black theologian must reject any conception of God which stifles black self-determination by picturing God as a God of all peoples. Either God is identified with the oppressed to the point that their experience becomes God's experience, or God is a God of racism. . . . Because God has made the goal of blacks God's own goal, black theology believes that it is not only appropriate but necessary to begin the doctrine of God with an insistence on God's blackness.[8]

Looking back on the history of Western civilization, I suppose the introduction of black liberation theology was inevitable. If you believe the lie that true Christianity is the white man's religion, then of course it becomes necessary to rewrite the Gospel and realign the Scriptures so that a new version of Christianity can become the black man's religion. If a person is angry enough, it will never occur to them that the new faith they've taken on looks nothing like the faith Jesus talked about, nothing like the hope Israel kept for thousands of years, and nothing like the freedom the Holy Spirit offers to all—slave and slaveowner alike.

As Brown's podcast wrapped up, I found myself feeling very sad for the woman on the panel. She was angry, and though she may have been angry about many things that ought to make us all angry, the sad part was that she had believed a lie that was keeping her from Jesus—not the white Jesus from the paintings or the militant black Jesus of her imagination, but the true Jesus who loves all people, black and white and every shade of brown.

Sadly, there are many people just like this poor woman. They have come to associate Christianity with whiteness—perhaps because something wicked was done to them in Jesus's name, or perhaps because they look around at a majority-white nation with a church that's also majority white and conclude that the Gospel must be for whites only. It's a sort of self-imposed religious Jim Crow law that keeps their hearts away from the truth—and it's infiltrated our culture in places we never would have imagined a few years ago.

In 2020, the National Museum of African American History and Culture at the Smithsonian Institute published a whiteness chart—a handy guide to help explain what "whiteness" is all about. Not only did the infographic include things like "objective, rational linear thinking" and "hard work" as aspects of whiteness, it also indicated that "Christianity is the norm" for white people.[9]

If Christianity were indeed a white man's religion, we would expect to find that over time, especially in our increasingly pluralistic society, fewer and fewer people of color putting their faith and trust in Jesus Christ. They should be walking away from the Lord in droves. But the numbers don't bear this out.

According to 2020 Census data, 30 percent of the U.S. population are white Protestants—that's 14 percent identifying as white evangelical Protestant and 16 percent identifying as white mainline Protestant.[10] When you consider that 75.5 percent of Americans are white,[11] that's roughly 40 percent of white Americans claiming Protestant Christian faith.

To be sure, that's not a small number, but let's compare it to the faith of black Americans. According to the same census data, black Protestants account for 7 percent of the U.S. population,[12] though black people in general make up 13.6 percent of the country.[13] That's 51.4 percent of black people in the Protestant tradition—11 percent more than white people.[14] And that's not even taking into consideration the roughly three million black Catholics in the United States.[15]

Clearly, most black Americans do not see the Gospel as a message that's only intended for white people. If it were simply a matter of assimilating into white culture, then we would expect much less segregation on Sunday morning. It seems, however, that despite what some want to believe, true Christianity—the faith handed down from the apostles—is a religion that can't be defined by a single race. As Billy Graham famously said during a crusade in South Africa, when the nation was still under apartheid: "Christ belongs to all people. He belongs to the whole world."[16]

☞

JESUS DEFINED HIS own mission when, one Saturday, He stood up in the synagogue in Nazareth and read from the scroll of Isaiah these words:

> The Spirit of the Lord is on me,
> because he has anointed me
> to proclaim good news to the poor.
> He has sent me to proclaim freedom for the prisoners
> and recovery of sight for the blind,
> to set the oppressed free,
> to proclaim the year of the Lord's favor. (Luke 4:18–19)

It's difficult to wrap our heads around it now, but many people who knew these words by heart centuries ago also insisted that the Bible supported the system of chattel slavery that was practiced in colonial America and, later, in the United States. They knew Jesus came "to set the oppressed free," and yet they kept their fellow human beings in chains, treated them like farm animals, forced them to work, and then deprived them of their wages. In their desire to continue profiting from a system that subjugated and abused men and women of color, they twisted the Christian faith into a weapon of unspeakable evil.

That's not to say there weren't devout Christians on the other side of the debate as well—abolitionists who knew that slavery could not stand under the weight of the true Gospel. In 1822, the Quakers became the first Christian denomination in England or the United States to officially oppose slavery, and as a movement, forbade its members from owning slaves.[17] And there were others from across the denominational spectrum who spoke out against American slavery. These faithful brothers and sisters knew that although a certain form of slavery existed in the Roman Empire of the first century, it had no place in the Kingdom of God. As people who have been called to live lives that echo Jesus's prayer—"Your will be done, on earth as it is in heaven" (Matthew 6:10)—followers of Jesus need to speak out against slavery. And so, in a Christian nation—as America claimed to be at that time—the practice would have to be abolished once and for all.

This was one of the great debates of the nineteenth century, and thankfully, those who recognized the evils of slavery and its incompatibility with the Christian faith prevailed. Nonetheless, that hasn't stopped people from pointing a finger back in time at Bible-toting slaveowners and declaring that Christianity must indeed be a white man's religion since it was used to do such immense harm to generation upon generation of African slaves.

Frederick Douglass, who was born a slave, was an aboli-
tionist, a statesman, and a vibrant Christian. He knew that
Jesus didn't favor one subset of humans terrorizing another.
He knew that, according to the Bible, all men were created
equal. And he knew there was something broken and twisted
in any version of Christianity that upheld a man's "right" to
own another man. In a famous speech delivered on July 5,
1852, Douglass said the following:

These ministers make religion a cold and flinty-hearted
thing, having neither principles of right action nor bow-
els of compassion. They strip the love of God of its beauty
and leave the throne of religion a huge, horrible, repulsive
form. It is a religion for oppressors, tyrants, man-stealers,
and thugs. It is not that "pure and undefiled religion"
which is from above, and which is "first pure, then peace-
able, easy to be entreated, full of mercy and good fruits,
without partiality, and without hypocrisy." But a religion
which favors the rich against the poor; which exalts the
proud above the humble; which divides mankind into two
classes, tyrants and slaves; which says to the man in chains,
stay there; and to the oppressor, oppress on; it is a religion
which may be professed and enjoyed by all the robbers
and enslavers of mankind; it makes God a respecter of persons, denies his fatherhood of the race, and tramples in
the dust the great truth of the brotherhood of man. All this
we affirm to be true of the popular church, and the popular worship of our land and nation—a religion, a church,
and a worship which, on the authority of inspired wisdom,
we pronounce to be an abomination in the sight of God.[18]

Douglass was able to love Jesus, treasure His Word, and
walk by His Spirit without stumbling over the hypocrisy of

much of the white American church of his day. He did not judge Jesus by the actions of His followers. Rather, he judged those who peddled wickedness and turned their gaze away from injustice according to the statutes of God he had learned in his personal study of the Bible. In short, he understood what Jesus meant when He said, "By their fruit you will recognize them" (Matthew 7:16).

Of course, Douglass wasn't the only black American in the days of slavery to embrace Christianity. Many slaves and former slaves bent their knee to Jesus Christ, recognizing that He brought freedom of another kind, even in the midst of earthly torment. And while it's true that some slave masters taught their slaves the Bible in the hope that certain passages, especially "Slaves, obey your earthly masters in everything" (Colossians 3:22), would keep them obedient, the evangelization of slaves was not always welcome. Part of the justification for enslaving members of the African race was that while Europe had largely embraced the Gospel, West Africa had not. Thus, the black people who were brought to America were seen as infidels and enemies of Christ, deserving of such judgment.[19] But if these slaves became brothers and sisters in the Lord, that argument would fizzle.[20]

Despite this hesitation to share the Gospel with black people, slaves en masse accepted Jesus Christ as their Lord and Savior, and despite having no official church affiliation, began praising the Lord in their own context. Negro spirituals were sung in the fields, Bible stories were shared orally, honest prayers rose to Heaven in the midst of tremendous pain, and when a slave had the opportunity to learn to read, the Scriptures served as their primer. These valiant, faith-filled Christians did not believe Christianity was the white man's religion. They saw in the open arms of Jesus eternal salvation and supernatural peace for their current circumstances.

☞

As Jesus slowly marched toward Golgotha, struggling under the weight of His own cross, He collapsed, unable to move any further. The Roman soldiers were not above beating condemned criminals for such things, but in this case, they didn't. Perhaps it was the hour or a rare instance of pity, but they let Jesus walk the rest of the way without His instrument of execution on His shoulders. To carry the load, these soldiers conscripted an innocent stranger from the crowd— Simon of Cyrene.

If you don't know your ancient geography, Cyrene was in North Africa, a region that would be part of Libya today. In all likelihood, Simon was a black man. While, in the moment, carrying Jesus's cross must have seemed a terrible inconvenience, even a demeaning or humiliating task, it proved to be one of the greatest honors ever bestowed upon a human being. And it seems that Simon eventually understood just what had been given to him.

Mark mentions that Simon was "the father of Alexander and Rufus" (Mark 15:21). It's a strange detail to include in the text. Most likely, it indicates that Alexander and Rufus were known to Mark's original audience. If they had become Christians, it could be because their father had, too.

Christianity was certainly not a white man's religion in the beginning. At the start, it was embraced exclusively by Middle Eastern Jews. But Simon and his sons show us that conversion to the Way of Jesus had nothing to do with skin color. At Pentecost, Jews from all over the known world— three thousand of them—accepted Peter's invitation to follow

Christ (Acts 2). On the road to Gaza, Philip explained the identity of Isaiah's Suffering Servant to an Ethiopian official, and he too grabbed hold of eternal life (Acts 8:26–40). After Cornelius and his household trusted Christ and were filled with the Holy Spirit (Acts 10), it became known that salvation had come to the Gentiles. Sometime later, the Lord Jesus appeared to Saul and commissioned him as an apostle to the Gentiles (Acts 9:1–19; 22:21). Paul and others took the Gospel to faraway places, preaching to Jews and to Gentiles, never once discriminating on the basis of skin color.

Jesus had told His disciples, "Therefore go and make disciples of all nations" (Acts 28:19)—and He didn't carve out an exception for dark-skinned people groups. God's heart is that all people everywhere might enter into His Kingdom (2 Peter 3:9), for He is creating one new people for His glory, a royal family in which "every nation, tribe, people and language" are included (Revelation 7:9).

This is central to the Gospel message. "For God so loved *the world*" (John 3:16, emphasis added). Not parts of the world, not certain people groups within it. He loves the whole world. All of us. That is why He sent His Son.

The early church struggled with this idea. When Gentiles began coming into the fold, Jewish Christians assumed that to be counted among God's people, they would have to follow the laws of Moses. But God's grace flowed into the lives of Greeks and Romans and anyone else who put their trust in the Jewish Jesus.

> So in Christ Jesus you are all children of God through faith, for all of you who were baptized into Christ have clothed yourselves with Christ. There is neither Jew nor Gentile, neither slave nor free, nor is there male and female, for you are all one in Christ Jesus. If you belong to Christ, then you

are Abraham's seed, and heirs according to the promise. (Galatians 3:26–29)

In one way or another, each of the Apostle Paul's letters dealt with racial divisions. This should bring us some comfort, because it's not a new problem that's arisen with us. It runs deeper than white and black. It goes back further than American sins. It's part of the battle our flesh wages against the Spirit of God at work within us. The following words were written about Jews and Gentiles, but they ring true of the racial divisions in the American church today:

> For he himself is our peace. . . . His purpose was to create in himself one new humanity out of the two, thus making peace, and in one body to reconcile both of them to God through the cross, by which he put to death their hostility. He came and preached peace to you who were far away and peace to those who were near. For through him we both have access to the Father by one Spirit. (Ephesians 2:14–18)

Jesus Christ is the only hope for humanity. As He Himself said, "I am the way and the truth and the life. No one comes to the Father except through me" (John 14:6). Therefore, for anyone to say that Christianity belongs to any one group it is a violent act of racism. Leading someone away from Christ with such a lie is worse than any physical attack one could perpetrate. Bruises heal and bones can be set, but a soul cannot save itself. We all need Him, and He stands ready to forgive every sinner who comes to Him in repentance—no matter the color of their skin.

CHAPTER 5

LIE #5: DEBT CAN BE CANCELED

The nine most terrifying words in the English language are:
"I'm from the government, and I'm here to help."
—Ronald Reagan

"There's no such thing as a free lunch."

While there's some debate over exactly where or how that saying began, in the late nineteenth century, many American tavern owners offered customers a free lunch whenever they ordered a drink.[1] The idea was simple: People lured in by the free lunch fare would then order several drinks—more than they ever would have if there were no food involved. So, while the food was technically complimentary, it only came with the required alcoholic beverage purchase. It wasn't really free; hence, the snarky expression that resulted and remains with us today.

The truth is, beyond the blessings of God, there's no such thing as a free anything. Everything of value costs someone something—whether it's lunch or a college education. There is no way for a debt or a bill simply to be canceled. The price always ends up on someone's balance sheet. And yet, there are people who still believe that debt can somehow be wiped out with the wave of a hand.

During the 2020 presidential campaign, Joe Biden began promising potential voters student loan forgiveness. At the time, he said all borrowers would see ten thousand dollars of their college loan debts canceled, while students who attended public universities or historically black colleges could receive up to $125,000 in forgiveness.[2] Exactly who would foot the bill for this debt-cancellation scheme was never a talking point at Biden's sparsely attended campaign events. Instead, the focus was on the relief the program would bring to millions of indebted college graduates. This left many people believing the debt would just disappear into the ether. No victims. No losers. Just peace and love with no more student loan repayment bills to pay. Kumbaya.

However, "there's no such thing as a free lunch." The bill for any student debt forgiveness program would be laid at the feet of the taxpayers. That's because the money received by students in the form of federal student aid loans was paid directly to colleges and universities when tuition was due. Therefore, that money has already been spent and is gone. All that remains now is the bill—so if the government were to cancel the debt, it would simply wind up in a different spot on the ledger sheet. It would still be a liability, and the missing money would need to be covered by tax revenue. Taxpayers nationwide would feel the burden—and most of those people either have already paid back their loans or did not sign an agreement to take on debt for their college education (or anyone else's) in the first place.

But none of this should come as a surprise. In the months following the Biden administration's attempt to enact a student-loan forgiveness program, economists and talking heads on cable TV offered up these same talking points ad nauseam. So let's go a bit deeper to understand how we got into this mess in the first place.

☞

IN DESCRIBING THE cost of being His disciple, Jesus told a simple parable:

> "Suppose one of you wants to build a tower. Won't you first sit down and estimate the cost to see if you have enough money to complete it? For if you lay the foundation and are not able to finish it, everyone who sees it will ridicule you, saying, 'This person began to build and wasn't able to finish.'" (Luke 14:28–30)

The lesson comes down to us today as a simple maxim for all kinds of endeavors, now divorced from following Jesus. "Count the cost," we say, and it still rings true as good advice. Only a fool buys something he cannot afford. Yet somehow, when it comes to college, nearly everybody does it. Unless a student gets a scholarship or comes from a particularly wealthy family, they don't have multiple six figures lying around the house to pay for four years of education. That's why, as of 2022, 55 percent of students who attended four-year public colleges and universities (and 57 percent attending private institutions) had student loans.[3] Each borrower owes an average of $37,172, and each household that has taken a student loan sits on $58,957 in student debt.[4] All told, the total amount of student debt in the United States is $1.75 trillion.[5]

So why do so many young adults sign on for debt? What makes college so attractive that they're willing to sign away a decade's worth or more of their future financial security to attend? In part, the answer is that, for many people, college is seen as a nonnegotiable. It's a pathway to the many, many jobs that are unavailable to someone wielding only a high school diploma. College graduates also tend to earn more money over the course of a lifetime—$1.2 million more than those without a bachelor's degree.[6] In some circles, blue-collar work might also carry a stigma, no matter how much money such jobs pay or how little the required training costs when compared to attending college. Then, of course, there's the peer pressure to attend school "like everyone else." It's difficult to underestimate the power of this kind of influence.

All of these factors combine to make college seem like it's absolutely necessary for some young people. In economic terms, college is relatively inelastic for these folks. That means their demand for college is affected little by the price, even if it rises sky-high. As a result, colleges and universities have little incentive to lower their prices and will find nearly any justification to raise tuition year after year. But that's not the only factor.

As Ronald Reagan famously said, "The nine most terrifying words in the English language are: 'I'm from the government, and I'm here to help.'"[7] The federal student aid program is indeed terrifying. In an attempt to "help" more students across this country attend colleges and universities, the federal government made access to student loan money incredibly easy.

It all started back in 1944 with the passage of the GI Bill. This move allowed veterans to attend school at no cost in most circumstances and for little cost in others. Few would argue that those who serve our country in the military shouldn't have educational opportunities provided for them when they return home. However, the GI Bill opened the door for the government to get further involved in higher education.

In 1958, federal legislators concerned that the Soviet Union would overtake us in fields important to national security and our progress as a nation, passed the National Defense Education Act, offering low-cost loans for qualified students who wanted to study mathematics, science, engineering, or education.

While there may have been some people—even many—in the federal bureaucracy who saw this act as a true "national defense" effort, the truth is it was unconstitutional. Nowhere in the U.S. Constitution is there a provision that allows the government to provide loans for education. And while many have been duped into believing the federal government is free to act so long as it's in the interest of the American people, the Tenth Amendment clearly states, "The powers not delegated to the United States by the Constitution, nor prohibited by it to the States, are reserved to the States respectively, or to the people."[8]

Of course, whenever the government starts a program, no matter the reason, it's difficult to end it. So, in 1965, the federal student loan program was expanded through the Higher Education Act, which provided Educational Opportunity Grants to help financially challenged students attend college. The Higher Education Act also instituted the Federal Family Education Loan Program (FFELP), which paved the way for banks and private lenders to offer government-subsidized and -guaranteed loans to students needing financial aid. To those not paying attention, it would have seemed the government was getting out of the loan business, but in reality, it was becoming a permanent fixture in the financial sector.

This sort of government overreach and expansion continued unabated for several more decades. In 1992, the government began lending directly to students in need. Some of those loans were unsubsidized—meaning students were responsible for the compounding interest even while they were still in school. In 2010, the Obama administration abolished the FFELP program so that all federal loans would come directly from the government rather than through private lenders.[9]

With each expansion came more money, more students borrowing, and more debt. As I've already mentioned, total student loan debt in this country now tops $1.75 trillion. In large part, this cascading debt is due to the amount of borrowed money the federal government has allowed to swamp the system. Like most goods, college comes at the price point people are willing to pay. Since nearly everyone has access to tens or even hundreds of thousands of dollars on some level, the price of college reflects that. In other words, colleges and universities adjust their prices to take advantage of the money that's available, nudging up prices year after year. And they will continue to do so as long as the federal government is willing to lend students just a little bit more and students are willing to take on more debt.

In a 1987 *New York Times* op-ed, then education secretary William J. Bennett wrote:

> If anything, increases in financial aid in recent years have enabled colleges and universities blithely to raise their tuitions, confident that Federal loan subsidies would help cushion the increase. . . . Federal student aid policies do not cause college price inflation, but there is little doubt that they help make it possible.[10]

It's a vicious cycle: Colleges charge a premium because students show up with lots of money available to them in the form of loans; the government willingly lends students increasingly more money to cover the rising cost of college; and students take on increasing amounts of debt because that's what college costs. And on and on it goes. If you flood a market with cash, then that cash is worth less and prices go up.[11] It's inflation, but isolated solely to higher education. That's why college prices have risen so much faster than inflation in the general economy. According to *Forbes* magazine, "The average cost of attending a four-year college or university in the United States rose by 497% between the 1985–86 and 2017–18 academic years, more than twice the rate of inflation."[12] That's because, as one study found, "a dollar increase in the subsidized cap and unsubsidized caps result in a 64-cent increase in sticker price."[13]

What's even scarier is that if the government were to "cancel" student loans, the net effect would be *even higher* prices for the next generation of borrowers. Remember: Colleges and universities receive their tuition money each time a student matriculates for a semester. The "canceled" student loans won't leave administrators in the lurch. In fact, it will simply incentivize them to keep expanding programs, campus amenities, and salaries, because they'll know they can simply keep raising prices. If there's ever a crisis, it's almost assured the government will bail students out again. At the same time, students will continue to borrow recklessly, because if the government canceled student loans once and got away with it, they'll do it again at some point.

Ronald Reagan was right: help from the government is terrifying.

☞

I REALIZE THAT what I've just described might lead some to conclude debt, especially student loan debt, is inevitable.

But in reality, we all have a choice. And yes, I know it's not fair—the choice set before the previous two generations was not so difficult. But I'm not talking about fairness; I'm talking about the wisdom to know which path to walk.

While the Bible never calls having debt a sin, it does call it "foolish," especially when it's avoidable. Consider this warning: "The rich rule over the poor, and the borrower is slave to the lender" (Proverbs 22:7). When you're in debt, you're a slave. Now, it may not be that you're legally owned by another human being, but your freedom is severely diminished nonetheless. Just ask anyone paying back hundreds of dollars every month for decades, attempting to dig out from their student loan nightmare.

Think of how that money might otherwise have been used. It could have gone to pay for the necessities of life—food, clothing, and shelter. It could have been invested so that it grew over time. It could have been used to start a business, learn new skills, or provide a cushion of security for tough times. And as Christians, let's not forget: We're called to give generously. In fact, Jesus said, "Give to everyone who asks you" (Luke 6:30). That's hard to do when you've got that big payment to make every month, servicing interest and ever so slowly paying down the principal.

Wisdom tells us we should avoid debt whenever possible. It's part of godly living. Again, it's not a direct sin to take on debt for a house or a college education or even a car, necessarily. But those who follow Jesus should also choose to follow the way of wisdom, and for every dollar borrowed, realize there's a trade-off in freedom. We're limited in what we can choose financially when part of our livelihood must go to service a debt.

With this in mind, the idea of magically canceling a debt seems like a temptation sent straight from Hell. It's a lie—and we know whom Jesus referred to as the father of lies (John 8:44). The enticement of easy money can lead people to make foolish choices. Just as Adam and Eve traded their freedom in the Garden of Eden for an easy route to wisdom (or at least that was what the devil told them), believing that debt can simply be written off and tossed aside will seduce some people into believing debt is really no big deal. It will blind them to the truth at the very moment they'll need to open their eyes and count the cost.

The Bible also says, "The wicked borrow and do not repay, but the righteous give generously" (Psalm 37:21). When Joe Biden or some other politician says that millions of people will be able to walk away from their student loan commitments, do we reckon that idea as "wicked"? The Bible does. When someone borrows money with a promise to repay, they are putting their reputation—their good name—on the line. And as Christians, we're also putting the name of Christ on the line. Make no mistake: we are called to represent Jesus here on Earth; that's part of what it means to be God's image-bearers (Genesis 1:27). How we live reflects upon the One we're supposed to be living for. So, when we give our word and say we will repay every penny we have borrowed according to the terms we have agreed to, and then we do not, we bring shame to our Lord and Savior.

The other side of Psalm 37:21 states things in a more positive light: "The righteous give generously." Why is that? Because the God we serve gives generously. "He causes his sun to rise on the evil and the good, and sends rain on the righteous and the unrighteous" (Matthew 5:45). And of course, the most gracious gift God gave to the world was His Son. "God demonstrates his own love for us in this: While we were still sinners, Christ died for us" (Romans 5:8). This is the heart of God—to lead rebellious people into His Kingdom and into

His family through kindness (Romans 2:4). Because God is so generous, He calls His people to be generous, too. But as anyone suffering under the weight of a large debt will tell you, it's awfully difficult to be generous when a significant amount of your income is already spoken for before you even receive your paycheck.

In case you were wondering if debt were only an Old Testament problem, Paul wrote in the New Testament, "Let no debt remain outstanding, except the continuing debt to love one another, for whoever loves others has fulfilled the law" (Romans 13:8). The second greatest commandment, according to Jesus, is that we love our neighbors (Matthew 22:39)—and that is the only debt we're supposed to carry with us throughout our lives. All others should be paid off so that we can be free to focus our time and energy on God's priorities.[14]

IN JUNE 2023, the U.S. Supreme Court ruled 6–3 that Biden's plan to cancel student loan debt for approximately forty-three million Americans was unconstitutional. Lawyers for the Biden administration had argued that the president, through the U.S. Department of Education, could unilaterally cancel student loans, citing a provision in the Higher Education Relief Opportunities for Students Act (HEROES):

> The law says the government can provide relief to recipients of student loans when there is a "national emergency," allowing it to act to ensure people are not in "a worse position financially" as a result of the emergency.[15]

The majority opinion was that the language of the HEROES Act was not specific enough. Chief Justice John

Roberts said precedent "requires that Congress speak clearly before a department secretary can unilaterally alter large sections of the American economy."[16] In other words, Congress drafts laws, not the president. But even that sentiment doesn't go far enough: Congress shouldn't be passing *any* laws outside of the jurisdiction enumerated by the Constitution. Shifting billions of dollars in debt from one group of Americans to another is not within the bounds of the government's responsibilities or authority.

I realize there is likely someone reading this book who was disappointed that Biden's vote-purchasing scheme—I mean, *student debt relief program*—was a bust. And I understand. It's human nature to want something that will bring a huge personal benefit, even if we know it's unfair to others and won't actually make society stronger. I also understand that getting out of debt is one of life's biggest challenges. However, no matter how much we might wish it were true, debt cannot be canceled; it can only be transferred.

There is simply no such thing as a free lunch.

CHAPTER 6

LIE #6: DISAGREEMENT MEANS WE CAN NO LONGER TALK

Out of difference can come the reinforcement of two important values. One is tolerance and the other is awareness that people who disagree over the things they hold dear really can live together in love and respect.

—Fred Rogers

A few months ago, I walked into the LEGO store at our local mall with my kids and looked around at the latest sets. Our family loves LEGOs. Over the years, we've spent hours together putting them together, making everything from castles to cars to spaceships. They're great toys.

But they're toys. And toys are for kids.

That's why I was so shocked when I saw a progress pride flag on the apron of one of the store's employees. But it wasn't just him—all four employees working at the store that day were prominently displaying pride flags on their uniforms.

I asked one of them why they were wearing a flag that promotes LGBTQ+ behavior in a toy store. Then I pulled out my phone and began recording.

It may seem like a small thing—a pin on an apron—but the messaging was anything but subtle. Just like a country's flag being staked on disputed territory, LGBTQ+ pride flags are displayed to show a certain territory has been claimed by advocates of that agenda. Apparently, LEGO wants the world to know where it stands. The problem is, they sell toys to children, some of whom are very young—so I wanted the world to know what the stores are promoting. I recorded a short video for social media. I pointed out what was happening, and I captured the responses of an employee who was more than happy to tell me children probably don't even know what the flag stands for.

That's how grooming starts: You introduce certain language, certain symbols, certain ways of doing things, to get kids comfortable with it. Later, when they are old enough to be confronted with an issue head-on, they're already predisposed to believe the lies that surrounded them when they were younger. So, no, it's not just a pin on an apron.

Within minutes, security was there to escort me and my children out of the LEGO store. And just so you know, we don't buy LEGOs anymore. We can find other toys—from companies that aren't actively promoting sexual perversion to children.

That short video I made that day soon went viral. I was glad that so many viewed the clip, not for my sake but for the attention it brought to LEGO's corporate "inclusion" policy. Several media outlets then picked up the video. Some of them understood where I was coming from as a father, and they had questions about this sort of political activism being aimed at children. Others—many others—criticized me for taking issue with the pride flag, speaking up, and hitting the record button. They called me a bigot, a homophobe, and worse. To be honest, I wear those criticisms like a badge of honor—not because any of them are true, but because it means I've rattled some folks on the radical left. They don't get upset unless you're speaking truth.

The next morning, I discovered that I had been locked out of my Twitter account. The message said my account would be restored when I removed the video of the LEGO store I had shared earlier. By that point, the video had been shared millions of times. There was no putting that genie back in the bottle. But that wasn't what the censors at Twitter really wanted. They knew it was too late to stop the clip from spreading around the globe. Their goal was to silence me and make me submit. The administrators at Twitter easily could have deleted the video on my feed without my knowledge or control—but they wanted me to do it to demonstrate they had power to control my words and actions. Eventually, I did take down the video to get my account back. But as I said, by that point it had already spread like wildfire and my message was out. I gave the tyrants what they wanted so I could move on with my life.

But that wasn't the only time I've been stifled on social media. I've been locked out, had my posts throttled, and been shadow-banned so that my posts reach just a handful of my tens of thousands of followers. This has happened only and always when I post something that upsets the sensibilities of the radical left, such as when I speak out against the murder of the unborn or the sexualization of schoolchildren in a provocative way. Someone behind the scenes at the offices of the social media platform gets offended and I get banned. By this point, I can almost tell before I post something if it's going to land me in Twitter jail.

But this is the world we now live in. If you disagree with someone, you silence them. It's not always as official as a social media lockout, but it's also not limited to cyberspace. Family members stop talking to each other because of politics. Churches split over tertiary issues. Employees are reprimanded by HR over their politically incorrect personal opinions.

There seems to be something in the air, something that has caused a large number of people to believe they have a right never to be offended. And if they are offended, it is their responsibility—nay, their duty—to shame and silence the person who offended them, even if the slight was unintentional. In this new world, intention and character no longer matter. All that seems to count is how the person on the receiving end feels.

But there is no human right not to be offended. If you were born into this world, at some point you will be offended. The question is, what will you do about it?

☞

ONE OF THE pillars our nation was built on is freedom of speech. In fact, it's the First Amendment to our Constitution, the number-one item on our Bill of Rights. That's how important it was to our Founding Fathers.

"Public opinion," [James Madison] wrote in the National Gazette, in December 1791, "sets bounds to every government, and is the real sovereign in every free one." But in a large republic such as the United States, it is "less easy to be ascertained, and . . . less difficult to be counterfeited." It was thus key, he argued, to facilitate "a general intercourse of sentiments," which included roads and commerce, as well as "a free press, and particularly a circulation of newspapers through the entire body of the people."

In Madison's view, a free republic depends ultimately upon public opinion. A Constitution could divide power this way and that, but in the end it is the people, and only the people, who rule. And for the people to rule wisely, they have to be able to communicate with one another—freely, without fear of reprisal. Thus, freedom of speech and press were not, for Madison, merely God-given rights. They were preconditions for self-government.[1]

The United States of America is supposed to be a nation of "We the people, by the people, and for the people." And so, Madison argued, we must have the ability to communicate with one another—to debate publicly and privately, to be able to freely persuade our neighbors to see our point of view. For a republic to function properly, no one can be silenced, canceled, or otherwise squelched. So, while the First Amendment prohibits the federal government from denying any citizen free speech, that's not enough. We, as Americans, must actively embrace freedom of speech for ourselves and others—even those who offend us.

Today many of us take the freedom to speak our minds for granted, as though it's a right we don't really need in our day. Some have even lost sight of what free speech is and what it's for. They behave as though it's more of a luxury—and a nuisance luxury at that. They tell us it might be best to restrict speech. In fact, in a 2021 study, 66 percent of college students said it was "acceptable to shout down a speaker" with whom they disagreed. Further, nearly one in four said using violence to stop a speech on campus should be permissible.[2] After all, "misinformation" is dangerous, they say. And the most important thing, they want us to believe, is that no one is offended, no one ever feels bad. Didn't your mother ever tell you, "If you don't have anything nice to say, don't say anything at all"? Our culture has come to view words as instruments of violence. Many now regard being offended to be the same as being abused.

Dr. David Bromell, a senior associate at the Institute for Governance and Policy Studies at Victoria University of Wellington, New Zealand, writes,

> In a free and open society, and in accordance with international human rights law, we have a right to protection from violence and from speech that intends or is imminently likely to incite violence and acts of hostility or discrimination.
>
> But we do not have a right to protection from disagreement, criticism, satire, offence or hurtful comments.
>
> Of course, words can hurt, but they do not hurt in the same way or to the same extent as sticks, stones, fists, knives or guns.
>
> Words are not weapons. Words are what we use instead of weapons, to express disagreement and assert our claims as we negotiate how to live together despite our differences, under the rule of law and without recourse to violence.
>
> If we equate words with weapons, we risk weapons being seen as no worse than words.[3]

Right now, we're living in a society that's more divided than it has been at any time in history except for the period immediately preceding the Civil War. This is not the time to shout each other down, huddle in our tribes, and hate one another. I'm not saying we need to forge some sort of false unity. Far from it. In fact, the very reason we need to speak freely to one another without fear of being silenced or canceled is because we *will* disagree.

Bromell continues:

In a diverse society where people want and value different things, I cannot reasonably expect other people to like, agree with, approve of, or affirm my ideas, beliefs, attitudes, values or way of life.

And just because someone criticises or disagrees with me does not necessarily mean they hate me. They just don't agree with me.

I have lived long enough to change my mind about a great number of things. Criticism and disagreement have played an important role in the evolution of what I think, feel and value.[4]

In the public square today, the Left controls nearly all of the mainstream media outlets—television, cable news, and what's left of the newspaper industry—much of Big Tech, most Hollywood studios, and the vast majority of colleges and universities. So it's not a stretch to say that progressives control the microphone. Is it any wonder, then, why they want to shut down the conversation? Not having the debate means you "win" it every time. But this sort of censorship and silencing of the opposition has trickled down so deeply into the soil of our culture that the weeds are threatening to choke the life out of our country. We have learned to silence one another (and ourselves) in believing the lie that disagreement equals hate.

As Bromell points out, it is in conversations, heated debates—and even in verbal fights—that we hone our ideas and even reconsider certain positions we've long held. Disagreement is healthy, not harmful. Scripture puts it this way: "As iron sharpens iron, so one person sharpens another" (Proverbs 27:17).

Logan Albright, director of research at the independent media production company Free the People, sees the rise of so-called "hate speech" as an epidemic, not because much of it is actually hateful but because we've allowed the word to permeate our culture:

> The word "hate" has simply become a rhetorical trick used to delegitimize opposing opinions and prevent us from having to honestly engage with the other side's point of view.
>
> Artists and entertainers describe those who don't like what they do as "haters" because it's easier to dismiss criticism as irrational than use it as an opportunity for self-improvement. Activists and ideologues use the same trick when they are insecure in their own positions and fear to intellectually engage with anyone not already in their camp. If you can ascribe hatred to your interlocutors, you don't have to answer what may be perfectly valid objections to your worldview; you don't even have to listen to them. What better way to maintain our bubbles of unanimity and moral certitude than to pretend everyone outside it is an evil misanthrope?
>
> But pretending something doesn't make it so, and the fact is that differences of opinion are not automatically accompanied by negative emotions. It is possible, contrary to a recent exchange I witnessed, to believe that biological sex is more than a social construct without being consumed by hate. It is possible to believe that less immigration would be good for the country without hating Hispanics. It is possible to believe in the preservation of traditional marriage and the nuclear family without hating gay people or single mothers. It is possible to question the morality of abortion without hating women.

I agree with some of the above positions and disagree with others, but I'm self-aware enough to recognize that deviation from my own position does not automatically constitute hatred for me and all the values I hold dear. In some cases, the other side might have compelling points that I need to address, or at least think about, before digging my heels in on my own point of view.[5]

By labeling a divergent viewpoint as "hateful," a person can move that argument into the category of "irrational" and unworthy of a response. No engagement necessary. Is it any wonder why it's become such a popular tactic? It isn't a new one either . . .

In the first century, the deacon Stephen, "a man full of God's grace and power" (Acts 6:8), was dragged before the Jewish ruling council known as the Sanhedrin to answer for his faith in Jesus. When it was his turn to speak, Stephen recounted Israel's history, showing how the people were stubborn and rebellious, rejecting the prophets God sent to show them the way. He then said, "And now you have betrayed and murdered [the Righteous One]" (Acts 7:52).

Of course, that upset the powerful religious leaders. "They were furious and gnashed their teeth at him" (Acts 7:54). But what really upset them was this:

> But Stephen, full of the Holy Spirit, looked up to heaven and saw the glory of God, and Jesus standing at the right hand of God. "Look," he said, "I see heaven open and the Son of Man standing at the right hand of God." (Acts 7:55–56)

At that, the Jewish religious leaders "covered their ears and, yelling at the top of their voices, they all rushed at him, dragged him out of the city and began to stone him"

(vv. 57–58). They couldn't stop Stephen from speaking—he wasn't about to shut up about Jesus just to please the who's who of Jerusalem's inner circle—so they plugged their ears and shouted at the top of their lungs to avoid hearing what Stephen had to say. That is, until a few minutes later when they stoned him to death.

I bring this up because it shows that something in our flesh recoils when we're confronted with a viewpoint that challenges our assumptions. The religious leaders didn't just send Stephen away because they disagreed with his theology, and they didn't just lock him up. They needed him silenced for good. Their twisted interpretation of the Law served as an excuse to torture to death a man they didn't like. They accused him of blasphemy—but are our cultural speech codes today so different? It seems calling someone a hater or a racist for something they said is the modern-day, secular equivalent of stoning them to death. Not to mention that, just like the Sanhedrin, so many of us believe it's acceptable to literally plug our ears and shout down those saying things we don't like in public places.

We serve a God who spoke creation into being. The Bible itself is a testament to the God who speaks, and we, as His image-bearers, have been given the power of speech. It's part of who we are. That's not to say someone with a speech impediment is somehow less human—nothing could be further from the truth! Rather, I mean that God is a speaking God, and we are a speaking people. To silence another image-bearer of God is, in a sense, to dehumanize them, to subjugate them; it's to insist that person is inferior in some way, that they are less than what God created them to be.

☞

THERE IS A better way, of course, a way of life that reveals we really can talk to each other—even love one another—when we disagree about core issues. At the very least, we should look to the example of Jesus. He disagreed with plenty of folks—religious leaders, tax collectors, prostitutes, and rich, young rulers—but He never shut down the conversations with them. He engaged, taught, argued, and even blessed those with whom He could not see eye to eye.

Now, I get it. You and I aren't Jesus. (He was never wrong! But sometimes we are.) We stumble and make mistakes. But that doesn't mean we can't emulate a life of courageous conversation, curious debate, and generous truth-telling. Famously, the late U.S. Supreme Court justices Antonin Scalia and Ruth Bader Ginsburg were close friends, even though they couldn't have been further apart on the political spectrum. Scalia was a champion of strict constructionist values while Ginsburg saw the need to interpret the Constitution anew for each generation. And yet they enjoyed each other's company. No doubt they talked politics from time to time—how could they not?—but they didn't let their disagreements build a wall between them:

> "Call us the odd couple," Scalia said of their relationship at a George Washington University event in 2015. "She likes opera, and she's a very nice person. What's not to like? Except her views on the law."
>
> At a time when the world seems so divided by bitter—and sometimes violent—partisan politics, the story of their unlikely friendship is a symbol of political bridge-building and old-school decency.
>
> The feminist "rock star" met the conservative justice in the early 1980s, when they both served as judges on the US

appeals court in Washington—and quickly learned they couldn't be more different.

Ginsburg was soft-spoken, petite and believed in a "living Constitution" that could evolve over time. Scalia, by contrast, was brash and burly and believed in strictly following the Constitution's original text. . . .

But away from the bench, the justices clicked, bonding over humor and a shared love of travel and wine.[6]

When Scalia passed away in 2016, Ginsburg said they were "best buddies."[7] Their shared love of opera even inspired an actual opera composed by Derrick Wang. Ginsburg referred to this in a written statement released after Scalia's passing:

Toward the end of the opera *Scalia/Ginsburg*, tenor Scalia and soprano Ginsburg sing a duet: "We are different, we are one," different in our interpretation of written texts, one in our reverence for the Constitution and the institution we serve. From our years together at the D.C. Circuit, we were best buddies. We disagreed now and then, but when I wrote for the Court and received a Scalia dissent, the opinion ultimately released was notably better than my initial circulation. Justice Scalia nailed all the weak spots—the "applesauce" and "argle bargle"—and gave me just what I needed to strengthen the majority opinion.[8]

Not only did Scalia and Ginsburg enjoy each other's company over their shared interests, but their disagreements strengthened their thinking on the job. A good argument can be helpful that way. Like a boxer who spars before the match, listening to those we disagree with actually prepares us to stand when it counts most.

Another odd couple has learned this firsthand: Robert P. George is a conservative thinker, legal scholar, and public philosopher. Cornel West is also a public philosopher, but he would categorize himself as a socialist and political activist. Yet the two men are good friends. Like Scalia and Ginsburg, on paper the two couldn't be further apart politically, but they have formed a bond that is far deeper than political issues. West says,

> I think it's, it's deeper than civility and it's even deeper than respect. I think we've got a genuine love for one another. I love this brother, I revel in his humanity. We've spent good time together. And so we just always want to send a sign to the nation that deep down in your heart, you know, love is not reducible to politics.[9]

George agrees:

> Well, I not only love Brother Cornel, I admire him, and I admire him for those virtues, for honesty and for integrity. He sets an example for me. He's inspiring to me. We may disagree about politics, but I do admire integrity—[he's a] person who says what he means, means what he says, who does not succumb to peer group pressure. Cornel has been under pressure from the progressive side sometimes to do things or say things that he actually doesn't agree with, and he refuses to yield. I try to do that on my end, and I look to him as a model for that.[10]

When asked how the two men could disagree without hating one another, George says it's a blessing to have friends with whom you disagree—and the most important component of those kinds of relationships is "intellectual humility":

Recognizing that we could be wrong about things. And someone we regard as goofy or misguided or bigoted might actually be right about those things. I could be wrong about values I cherish. I could be wrong about identity-forming beliefs for myself. But the only way I'm going to figure out whether I'm right or wrong is to listen to somebody who has a different point of view, and challenge. The reason I don't shout at Cornel. . . . I'm not going to learn anything from somebody I'm shouting at. I'm just not. There's not going to be any learning in that conversation. I want to learn from Cornel. He has things to teach me, I have things to learn, even when he's wrong about some things. I want to know what his reasons are because they're gonna deepen and enrich my understanding, even if . . . he's not actually correct. So if we're shouting, if we're not listening to each other, there's not gonna be any learning.[11]

At the end of the day, free speech is all about the search for truth and meaning. If we shut each other down, we'll never advance. Cornell Law School dean Jens David Ohlin notes, "I firmly believe that the need for civility increases proportionally as our disagreements become sharper. . . . It is when we disagree that we must strain to engage with each other in ways that are both productive and broad-minded."[12]

As Christians, we know the Truth—His name is Jesus Christ—and we have the Bible, of which every last word is true. But that doesn't mean we don't need to argue. Look at the example of Paul in Athens. He "reasoned in the synagogue with both Jews and God-fearing Greeks, as well as in the marketplace day by day with those who happened to be there" (Acts 17:17). While he was doing this, "a group of Epicurean and Stoic philosophers began to debate with him" (v. 18).

This led to an invitation to address a session of the Areopagus (see vv. 19–34).

As we listen to others, we earn and we learn. We *earn* the opportunity to speak, but we also *learn* where those with whom we disagree are coming from. Of course, listening is not merely a means to an end. Nothing is more insufferable than a person who pretends to listen but never really engages. Rather, we listen because we respect the humanity of the person we're arguing with. Speaking, listening, debating, and at times, even outright fighting with our words is how we engage the culture where God has placed us. And it's one of the ways we love our neighbors.

☞

IN THE LITTLE one-chapter book of Jude, tucked in the back of the New Testament, we read these simple but important words:

> Dear friends, although I was very eager to write to you about the salvation we share, I felt compelled to write and urge you to contend for the faith that was once for all entrusted to God's holy people. (Jude 3)

We are to "contend for the faith." The Greek word used there by the half-brother of our Lord means to "make a strenuous effort on behalf of, struggle for."[13] We can't sit around in a holy huddle and assume the outside world hears us and understands our message. We need to contend. We need to fight, not with our fists or weapons of war, but with the truth. And if we believe that we carry words of life—the words of Jesus (John 6:68)—given to us by God the Father, we cannot participate in the silencing of anyone, no matter how strongly we might disagree, for then, we too will be silenced.

CHAPTER 7

LIE #7: TRANSGENDER PEOPLE
ARE UNDER ATTACK

*I'm not obsessed with gender. I'm obsessed with
the preservation of a functional society. Ours will fail
if we allow some to impose their personal fictions on others.*
—Bret Weinstein

At eleven minutes past ten on the morning of March 27, 2023, gunshots rang out in the ordinarily quiet Green Hills neighborhood of Nashville, Tennessee. The glass exploded on a set of side doors at The Covenant School, allowing Audrey Hale to enter the building, armed and ready to kill.

Covenant is a private Christian elementary school operated by Covenant Presbyterian Church, serving students from pre-kindergarten through sixth grade. No one in the building that day was a threat to Hale. They were children who had come to learn and teachers who had come to provide instruction. It's hard to think of a more peaceful environment. But Hale turned the school into a living nightmare. For fourteen minutes, she went unchallenged, free to roam the halls and pursue her victims, gunning them down without mercy.

In total, Hale fired more than 150 rounds from two rifles and a handgun. She murdered three children—Evelyn Dieckhaus, William Kinney, and Hallie Scruggs, all age nine—and three adults: substitute teacher Cindy Peak and custodian Mike Hill, both sixty-one; and the sixty-year-old headmistress, Katherine Koonce. Who knows how many more innocent lives would have been snuffed out had Metro Nashville Police officers Rex Englebert and Michael Collazo not intervened? Bodycam footage shows the two men storming the building and firing upon Hale, who then dropped to the ground, lifeless.

Those two officers ended what can only be described as a massacre.

It's hard to imagine a more horrifying scene. As the minute hand clicked past ten o'clock that morning, it was a normal school day. Older kids squirmed in their desks while listening to morning announcements before rehearsing the multiplication table. Kindergarteners gathered in a circle on the carpet for storybook time. The cafeteria crew made macaroni and cheese and tater-tots in preparation for the coming lunch rush. And then, with the sound of gunfire, everything changed. Six people lost their lives, and everyone else lost their sense of peace and security. In fact, it's likely life will never be the same again for the survivors, not to mention the parents and loved ones of everyone who was there that day.

This nation has seen mass shootings before—from Columbine in 1999 to West Nickel Mines in 2006 to Sandy Hook in 2012 and hundreds more besides. This type of violence has become a sad fact of our age. Whenever someone walks into a school with a firearm to target children, it's an act of pure evil. Ordinarily, the media condemns these sick and twisted individuals who murder children. There are debates about what's causing these incidents, but the perpetrators are never defended or given center stage as if they are victims.

But then there was Audrey Hale.

A short time after she was identified as the killer, the Trans Resistance Network released a statement, which said, in part, "Hate has consequences":[1]

> We point out that today's incident in Nashville, TN [sic] is not one tragedy, but two. . . .
>
> The second and more complex tragedy is that Aiden or Audrey Hale, who felt he had no other way to be seen than to lash out by taking the life of others, and by consequence, himself.
>
> We do not claim to know the individual or have access to their inner thoughts and feelings. We do know that life for transgender people is very difficult, and made more difficult in the preceding months by a virtual avalanche of anti-trans legislation, and public callouts by Right Wing personalities and political figures for nothing less than the genocidal eradication of trans people from society.[2]

And, of course, the Trans Resistance Network made sure to use its moment of publicity to chastise the media for using Hale's chromosome-determined pronouns and birth name:

> We remind the news media to respect the self-identified pronouns of transgender individuals who come across your desk. Aiden Hale self identified [sic] with "He, Him" pronouns on forward facing sites.[3]

Mainstream media outlets began parroting these talking points, highlighting the difficult lives transgender people often live and painting conservatives as hate-filled bigots. Several sources apologized for initially "misgendering" Hale as a woman and using the pronouns "she" and "her."[4] The *New York Times* noted how rare it is for a mass shooting to be perpetrated by a female—and then later corrected the record, insisting that Hale was, in fact, male.[5]

A police investigation revealed more firearms and a manifesto at Hale's home. As of this writing, the manifesto has not been released to the public, so I cannot say with any certainty what the document would reveal about Hale's motives or underlying mental condition. However, it is indeed suspicious that the document has been kept from the public. While some speculate it is merely a list of personal grievances and therefore not germane to her identity as a transgender person,[6] that hardly seems likely. If that were the case, police could certainly disclose the nature of the writings without providing any of the details, maintaining the privacy of anyone mentioned while satisfying public interest. And while many would doubt the truth of such a statement, were it to be issued, the authorities would be on the record. But they are not. Not only do the FBI and other law enforcement agencies refuse to release the actual document, they also refuse to describe it in any manner. To me, that seems more like legal maneuvering than anything else, because their silence preserves deniability in a court of law. No one's lying exactly; they're just not telling us the truth. Or much of anything else.

It is much more likely that the manifesto does indeed contain a political justification for the mass murder. Hale had been planning the shooting for some time—police admit that much.[7] This wasn't a spur-of-the-moment, rage-filled attack fueled by a passing wave of uncontrollable emotional distress. It wasn't random; it was deliberate and methodical.

What makes this case particularly strange is that The Covenant School parents have taken legal action to ensure police never release it. While their motivations for this are unclear, what is clear is that the privacy being afforded to a deceased mass murderer is unprecedented:

> Tennessee's victims' rights statute does not give individuals a "carte blanche" to veto other laws, such as the one that allows people the right to public records, said Deborah Fisher, executive director of the Tennessee Coalition for Open Government.
>
> "There's nothing really to indicate that there would be this ability for victims to veto the release of otherwise public records and in, and in this case, crime records," Fisher said Thursday.
>
> Fisher is not a party in the ongoing litigation over whether Hale's writings—previously described as a "manifesto"—should be released.
>
> But she was asked by an attorney involved to provide her input on the history of the victims' rights legislation, she said.
>
> "In this case, the perpetrator is dead," she went on, "but if the shooter had gone to trial, most likely the writings of the shooter would be part of the evidence in the case about motivation."
>
> "I don't think that in that situation, the victims could veto those being submitted in a public trial, and I don't think that they can veto them being released as crime evidence in a case that doesn't go to trial because the person is dead," added Fisher, who is also director of the John Seigenthaler Chair of Excellence in First Amendment Studies at Middle Tennessee State University.[8]

Hale's words are being shielded from public view. She is being treated as though she were just another victim of that tragic morning in March 2023. Worse than that, blame for the entire massacre is, by inference, being placed on the shoulders of conservatives, especially Christians, who oppose so-called "trans rights." Just so we're clear, these include but are not limited to: a child's right to self-select a gender, the right of young girls to have their breasts removed, the right of young boys to have their penises cut off and discarded as medical waste, and the right to hormone therapy for anyone claiming to be living in the wrong body—sometimes at taxpayer expense.

In our culture today, victimhood has tremendous power. Therefore, we shouldn't be surprised that nearly everyone wants to play the victim card. But let's be clear about what we're talking about: Up until about five minutes ago, everyone agreed there were two, and only two, genders. And while appearance was always a good indicator of a person's gender, their genitalia were the real decider. Barring that, at the cellular level, the presence of a Y chromosome marked a male, while XX marked a female. But now, if you insist that a woman is a woman or a man is a man, contrary to the way that person chooses to identify, you're a hate-filled bigot. With these rules, the story writes itself: "Transgender folks are attacked relentlessly, just for being who they are!"

AT THE BEGINNING of time, God created human beings. The Bible says,

> So God created mankind in his own image, in the image of God he created them; male and female he created them. (Genesis 1:27)

That seems like an unnecessary detail to include. Of course He created them "male and female." How else would He have created them? It's almost as if God looked down through history and saw our current moment, face-palmed, and then said to Himself, "You know what? I'm going to spell it out for them. Male and female. Just two genders. Nothing in between. No switching. It doesn't get any clearer than that." And just in case we somehow missed it in Genesis, Jesus confirms this same truth for us in the New Testament: "At the beginning of creation God 'made them male and female'" (Mark 10:6).

When a person decides God was wrong about the gender He gave them, they take on a posture of rebellion. And when they take steps to "change" their gender, they are mutilating God's image, which they were made to carry. Proponents of transgender ideals believe a person is really only who they are on the inside; the body is nothing more than a shell. In this way, walking around in a body is really no different than driving around in a car. So, if the spirit within a person feels they are a different gender, then what's wrong with taking their body in to the surgeon for an overhaul? Why drive a Kia if you think you belong in a Subaru? No sense driving around in a car that doesn't fit the real you. But the Bible never downplays the human body as just a shell.

Our bodies are part of God's good creation, and even though they are subject to decay in this sinful world, they will one day be resurrected in glory. In that way, our bodies will remain an essential part of who we are throughout eternity. Not only that, but the Son of God "became flesh and made his dwelling among us" (John 1:14). Fully God, the Son became fully human as well. And when He rose from the dead, it was with a body. Glorified though it was, it was still His earthly body—the same body that grew in Mary's womb. When He ascended to the right hand of the Father, it was in His body. Except for that brief period between the Crucifixion and the Resurrection, He never discarded His flesh once He took it on.

All that should tell us something about the goodness of our bodies. They're not merely cars we drive around in. They're not shells to be adorned or vandalized as we see fit. They are part of our humanity and a gift from God.

Back in Genesis, God went further. He said that, as male and female, we are to "be fruitful and increase in number" (Genesis 1:28). That's part of our task as God's image-bearers, part of our role as His children. It's in our DNA to be fruitful and multiply. That doesn't mean that a couple who can't have children because of a health problem or a medical issue are any less image-bearers of God. But when a person takes hormone blockers and has their genitals removed, they're desecrating the holy role God has given them. They are harming themselves not only physically, but spiritually and psychologically as well.

This is why God's people oppose the LGBTQ+ agenda with its emphasis on self-identification and the use of drugs and surgeries to "change"[9] a person's gender. Not only is it an affront to God and His good creation, but it's harmful to the people who embrace it, including children, who are often pressured into making decisions they are not mature enough to make— decisions that forever alter their lives and mar their bodies.

But aren't there people who honestly believe they were born in the wrong body and, as a result, are plagued with feelings of depression and suicide? Wouldn't it be better to let these people alter their body to better align it with their feelings? These are the sorts of questions that deep-feeling, kindhearted people ask. After all, few of us actually want to see our neighbors in pain or watch them endure a lifetime of misery. Transgender activists know this, which is why they will tell the parents of a confused little boy, "Would you rather have a dead son or a living daughter?"

With a stark choice like that, how could anyone oppose their "treatment plan"?

In their insightful booklet "Exposing the Gender Lie: How to Protect Children and Teens from the Transgender Industry's False Ideology," Jeff Myers and Brandon Showalter write:

> Nobody is truly "trans" in any meaningful, ontological sense because it is impossible to be born in the wrong body, and no one can change their sex. A person may, indeed, suffer from body dysmorphia of some kind, and there are many kinds of dysmorphia, including muscle dysmorphia (a belief that one's muscles are too small) and anorexia (a distorted perception of body weight). People experiencing these things ought to be treated with the utmost care and compassion. All humans are either male or female. To be "transgender" is, at most, a self-determined identity construct based on a set of cultural, sex-based stereotypes not rooted in biology.[10]

As I hope you are beginning to realize, much of the debate surrounding transgender issues has to do with the nature of reality and the meaning of certain words. Transgender advocates want to separate biological sex (which cannot be changed) from gender (which, they insist, is up to the individual and can be fluid). Language often becomes a weapon, as the enforcement of preferred pronouns is used to coerce agreement with the transgender narrative. Part of that narrative is that many transgender people will simply not be able to make it through this life without proper medical intervention. However, as Myers and Showalter point out:

> Activists insist that even young children and pre-pubescent youth can know that they have the wrong body and that

their "gender identity" struggles can be resolved through risky experimental medical procedures. Trans ideologues routinely claim that these procedures are necessary to curb self-destructive behavior, including the possibility of suicide.

These treatments allow patients, including young children, to alter their endocrine systems with hormone blockers, followed by synthetic opposite sex hormones, and then perhaps surgery that irreparably alters their secondary sex characteristics.

But it is all a lie. Biological sex is immutable. Medical interventions—such as blockers, hormones, and surgery—produce grave harm as they attempt to circumvent biology in pursuit of a physical impossibility. In many ways, this is also a child abuse scandal, since children cannot give adequate informed consent to the medicalization which yields such dire repercussions. Worse still, many of the young people who have embraced a trans identity and are being steered down this destructive medical pathway are already dealing with one or more mental health challenges that can be left unaddressed in the rush to treat symptoms of gender dysphoria rather than its causes.[11]

A study conducted in May 2022 found that most Americans—64 percent—support laws that would shield transgender people from discrimination, and 60 percent believe a person's gender is determined at birth and cannot change. That last number is up from 54 percent in 2017. That means that even as Americans are sympathetic toward people who believe they are transgender, they are growing increasingly skeptical of the transgender narrative being foisted upon them.[12] But rather than allowing our nation's citizens to have an honest debate on the topic, the federal government and the mainstream media insist on declaring "the truth" to us, silencing the opposition, and claiming the moral high ground. But they're presenting a twisted reality.

In fact, that reality is more than twisted—it's fabricated, says Dr. Riittakerttu Kaltiala, head of the department of adolescent psychiatry at Finland's Tampere University Hospital. In a November 14 article published by The Free Press, she wrote that she helped establish her nation's "gender identity services" model based on a 2011 Dutch paper saying that mentally healthy boys who insisted from a young age that they were girls could transition more easily and credibly by receiving hormone blockers and surgery at younger ages. But once "gender-affirming clinics" were established throughout Europe, Kaltiala says she found the opposite to true: Ninety percent of the young patients who came flocking to them for help were female, and most suffered from "severe psychiatric conditions."[13]

> Remarkably, few had expressed any gender dysphoria until their sudden announcement of it in adolescence. Now they were coming to us because their parents, usually just mothers, had been told by someone in an LGBT organization that gender identity was their child's real problem, or the child had seen something online about the benefits of transition.
>
> Even during the first few years of the clinic, gender medicine was becoming rapidly politicized. Few were raising questions about what the activists—who included medical professionals—were saying. And they were saying remarkable things. They asserted that not only would the feelings of gender distress immediately disappear if young people start to medically transition, but also that all their mental health problems would be alleviated by these interventions. Of course, there is no mechanism by which high doses of

hormones resolve autism or any other underlying mental health condition. ...

The young people we were treating were not thriving. Instead, their lives were deteriorating. We thought, *what is this?* Because there wasn't a hint in studies that this could happen. Sometimes the young people insisted their lives had improved and they were happier. But as a medical doctor, I could see that they were doing worse. They were withdrawing from all social activities. They were not making friends. They were not going to school. We continued to network with colleagues in different countries who said they were seeing the same things.[14]

In 2015, Kaltiala and her fellow clinicians even published a paper describing what they were seeing among transitioners. But rather than curbing the issue, sexual activists doubled down on it. While Finland eventually put measures in place to help disturbed children get the psychiatric care they actually needed, the scientifically unsound activism is still rolling across the United States in waves. Kaltiala wrote,

Your first pediatric gender clinic opened in Boston in 2007. Fifteen years later there were more than 100 such clinics. As the U.S. protocols developed, fewer limitations were put on transition. A Reuters investigation found that some U.S. clinics approved hormone treatments at a minor's first visit. The U.S. pioneered a new treatment standard, called "gender-affirming care," which urged clinicians simply to accept a child's assertion of a trans identity, and to stop being "gatekeepers" who raised concerns about transition. ...

... I have been particularly concerned about American medical societies, who as a group continue to assert that children know their "authentic" selves, and a child who declares a transgender identity should be affirmed and started on treatment. (In recent years, the "trans" identity has evolved to include more young people who say they are "nonbinary"—that is, they feel they don't belong to either sex—and other gender variations.)

Medical organizations are supposed to transcend politics in favor of upholding standards that protect patients. However, in the U.S. these groups—including the American Academy of Pediatrics—have been actively hostile to the message my colleagues and I are urging.[15]

These issues are not just ideas; they have real-world consequences. On March 31, 2023, William Whitworth was arrested for planning an attack similar to Hale's on schools and churches in Colorado. Whitworth identifies as female and goes by the name "Lily."[16] Writing for the *Washington Examiner* after the events at Covenant School and Whitworth's arrest, Christopher Tremoglie explained how the Biden administration has not only gotten things wrong—it's obscured the truth to advance its pro-LGBTQ+ agenda:

> The Biden administration is lying to the public, and it has been doing so for quite some time. Inflammatory rhetoric, exaggerated claims, and incendiary remarks were all used to create false narratives to frighten transgender people, and their ardent supporters, into thinking that they are in danger in this country. Nothing could be further from the truth.
>
> There aren't any records of anyone taking weeks to plan to assassinate transgender children. No one has committed any terrorist acts targeting children experiencing gender confusion. But do you know who has suffered such tragedies? Christian children. . . .

Biden has abandoned all truth, decency, and integrity in advancing a cult-like, hyperbolic, and hysterical narrative that is used to create an environment of fear and to justify violence. Christians, who are legitimately being targeted, hunted, and killed, are left to fend for themselves.[17]

In May 2021, a fifteen-year-old "gender-fluid" boy wearing a skirt forcibly sodomized a female classmate in the girls' lavatory at Stone Bridge High School in Loudoun County, Virginia. Rather than being arrested and tried for his crime, the male student was transferred to Broad Run High School, also in Loudoun County, where he sexually assaulted another female student.[18]

The rapist was eventually tried in juvenile court (while once again wearing a skirt),[19] and Loudoun County Public Schools superintendent Scott Ziegler and public information officer Wayde Byard were indicted for their handling of the situation.[20] But the question persists: Why was a rapist protected and students left in harm's way? While we may never have an official answer, it seems clear that the boy's gender fluidity and the school system allowing him to freely enter the girls' restroom are the distinctives in this case.

I bring up this case—and the others—not to imply that every transgender person is a murderer or a rapist waiting to snap. However, these incidents highlight the mental condition of people who are confused about their gender—and the lengths to which public officials are willing to go in order to avoid offending the wokerati. Until 2013, the American Psychiatric Association's *Diagnostic and Statistical Manual of Mental Disorders* (DSM), the go-to volume for defining and classifying mental health disorders, included "gender identity disorder." That last word—"disorder"—is important, because it means that a person who struggles to accept their biological gender has a mental health problem. But with the introduction of the DSM-5, "gender identity disorder" was replaced with "gender dysphoria":

> [The APA] did so in the hopes that it would "avoid stigma and ensure clinical care for individuals who see and feel themselves to be a different gender" than the one they were born as. People with GD feel like they don't belong in their bodies. They may even feel a sense of disgust with their genitals. This leads them to want to live as the opposite sex, or as transgender.
>
> The APA goes on to say that "it is important to note that gender nonconformity is not in itself a mental disorder. The critical element of gender dysphoria is the presence of clinically significant distress associated with the condition."
>
> By replacing the word disorder with dysphoria, the organization hoped to help remove the stigma that the person is "disordered." The APA states that "the changes regarding gender dysphoria in DSM-5 respect the individuals identified by offering a diagnostic name that is more appropriate to the symptoms and behaviors they experience without jeopardizing their access to effective treatment options."[21]

Essentially, the APA changed terms in order to change outcomes. Gender identity disorder has a root cause—one that, if discovered, can free the sufferer from a mental health problem by helping them accept their biological gender. But "gender dysphoria" flips the script; now, the problem is not that a person believes they are the wrong gender (and should be living as the opposite sex) but that it is uncomfortable and stressful for them to live in the "wrong" body. Therefore, the correct "treatment" is to do whatever is necessary to make them more comfortable in their skin—surgery, hormones, puberty blockers, ensuring the rest of the world changes its language, and so forth.

In order for a male to have approximate female genitalia, the penis is removed and an incision is made in the scrotum. Then the testicles are removed and the urethra is shortened. Next, "excess" skin is used to create makeshift labia and a vagina, which of course can never actually function in the same manner as a biological female's. The "vagina" is really a wound that is never allowed to close up and heal. Estrogen supplements stimulate the growth of breasts to complete the look.[22] While this whole procedure would give Dr. Frankenstein a run for his money, the female-to-male surgical transition procedure is more gruesome still.

To create the likeness of male anatomy, a woman must have her breasts, uterus, and ovaries surgically removed. Sometimes hormones are used to artificially enlarge the clitoris so that it can be used as a penis, but more often a skin graft taken from an arm or thigh is used to construct one. This, of course, leaves the patient noticeably scarred in the place where the flesh was taken. And no matter what anyone might want to believe, that person will never have an actual penis—just a phallus composed of tissue borrowed from another part of the body, never at home between their legs. Male hormones are used to stimulate hair growth on the face and chest.[23] And the image of God with which that person was created is forever marred.

In 2016, a bill was making its way through the North Carolina House of Representatives. It was called the Public Facilities Privacy & Security Act, or House Bill 2 (HB2), and was meant to restrict bathrooms in public facilities, including schools, to men or women based on their biological gender at birth.[24]

At the time, it was shocking to think that we needed such a law—that we needed to codify men's rooms and ladies' rooms. But we did. We needed to protect the vulnerable by preserving restroom privacy. As you can imagine, though, there was a vigorous debate over the bill, with LGBTQ+ activists calling it discriminatory and concerned parents calling it a necessity.

In the days before the vote, I went to the North Carolina General Assembly to support the bill. But so did many other people. The legislature gave fifteen people from each side of the debate a few minutes to speak. They lined us up in the order in which we would appear before the body. To make sure it was fair, they alternated between people supporting the bill and those opposing it, back and forth, until everyone had the opportunity to voice their concerns. Therefore I stood between two transgender people as I awaited my turn to speak.

Thankfully, the proceedings were civil. There was no violence to speak of. I got to say my piece, and the bill ended up passing a few days later.[25] What I remember most about the day I stood up before the general assembly, however, wasn't what I said or what I heard. It wasn't the feeling in the room or the sight of protestors outside of the building. It was the smell.

I don't say that to be mean, the way a child would tell another child on the playground that they smell like dirty socks. I mean, the post-op men in drag I stood next to in line actually, literally stank. The scent is difficult to describe. The closest thing I can think of is the smell inside a nursing home when a bedridden and very ill octogenarian is within days of dying. It's the stench of death—and it stuck to those men like a terrible cologne they couldn't wash off. From what I understand, it comes from having an open wound serving as a false vagina where their penis used to be. The bacteria from the sore, combined with sweat, creates a disgusting cocktail of foulness that clings to the man. Ironically, their attempt to appear more feminine means they end up smelling more like animals.

In the Bible, God says sinful people "are smoke in my nostrils, a fire that keeps burning all day" (Isaiah 65:5). Sin is like a stench that rises up to the heavens. It stinks. We have to be washed in the blood to remove it. And while I understand that all sin is like that to God, I can't help but think there's something fitting about the fact that attempting to thwart God's good gift of gender results in a horrible, rancid scent from which a person can't easily escape.

The purpose of this chapter is to combat the lie that transgender people are somehow under attack from Christians. And while I believe that society protects, shields, and affirms gender-confused people in unhealthy and unhelpful ways, it actually is true that transgender men and women are under attack; it's just not in the way they tell us. The truth is, they are under attack from themselves and from our LGBTQ-saturated culture.

In 2018, public health researcher Lisa Littman published a peer reviewed article in an academic journal examining the phenomenal rise of teens identifying as transgender. Her findings revealed that 63.5 percent of young girls who had self-identified as transgender during their adolescence did so after being immersed in social media for extended periods of time:

> Parents describe that the onset of gender dysphoria seemed
> to occur in the context of belonging to a peer group where
> one, multiple, or even all of the friends have become gender

dysphoric and transgender-identified during the same timeframe. Parents also report that their children exhibited an increase in social media/internet use prior to disclosure of a transgender identity.[26]

While Littman's is a single study, and one that does not purport to explain the entirety of the recent surge in transgender identification, it does reveal that people are susceptible to the culture by which they are surrounded.[27] It certainly pokes holes in the Left's narrative that transgender people have always existed in large numbers but were just too afraid to come out of the shadows due to cisgender, heteronormative oppression. What seems more likely is what the Bible warned us about nearly two thousand years ago—that we have gone so far down the road of depravity that we must now "invent [new] ways of doing evil" (Romans 1:30).

But rather than addressing the root cause of their confusion and depression, people with gender identity disorder are sold a bill of goods that costs a fortune and forever alters their anatomies. Just think about all that is required for a person to undergo sex reassignment protocols—the surgeries and the hormone therapies. This generally takes several years, multiple surgeries, and well over $100,000 per person.[28] And there's no going back, so once a person chooses this path, they cannot turn around and go the other way. Just ask the handful of "detransitioners" who are now speaking out about what they experienced and why they regret it.

"No matter how much information they would have given me as a child, I just would not have been able to consent to this," nineteen-year-old Chloe Cole told a federal House subcommittee in July 2023 about the permanent health problems she incurred while seeking to become a male, starting at age twelve. "And my parents were required to sign off on these, but it was under duress. I don't think it was really consent. It was coercion. They were told they were going to face the false dichotomy of either your child transitions or she dies. But transition almost killed me. And the evidence suggests that is a common practice."[29]

As a Christian pastor, I stand up proudly and repeat the words of Scripture:

> So God created mankind in his own image, in the image of
> God he created them; male and female he created them.
> (Genesis 1:27)

I make no apologies for repeating the truth and proclaiming it wherever I can. It's not because I hate transgender people or want to see them depressed or suicidal. Rather, it's because I know the freedom they are looking for cannot be found at the tip of a surgeon's scalpel or at the bottom of a bottle of hormone pills. It can only be found in Jesus Christ. He has the power to set a person free from the confusion that overtakes them to the point of self-mutilation. He can renew their mind, transform their heart, and give them hope and a future. And He wants to.

I don't know what Audrey Hale was thinking on the morning of March 27, 2023. We haven't been able to see her manifesto, so none of us has a clear picture of that. But she attacked children and faculty at a Christian school she had attended as a young girl. That wasn't by accident. She murdered people who love Jesus, people who believe as I do—that Jesus Christ is the only way any of us can be set free from what binds us, regardless of what form it takes.

In my opinion, the most dangerous part of the identity cult—no matter where one finds themselves on the LGBTQ+ spectrum—is that tying one's identity to sexual preference or gender means any questions or debates related to their life-style will feel like a personal attack.[30] In this way, these people are blind to the truth and see attacks where there is only concern and love. The truth is, transgender people may have marred their bodies to obscure the image of God, but they are still made in His image—and He can set them free. That is the Christian hope in the midst of the mess in which we currently find ourselves.

WARNING

The following chapter contains direct quotations from young adult and children's books that are pornographic and sexually explicit in nature. Much of the content that follows is therefore inappropriate for children, as well as adults with a sensitive or God-fearing constitution.

CHAPTER 8

LIE #8: IF YOU'RE AGAINST PORNOGRAPHY, YOU'RE A BOOK-BANNER

*The day that any parent cannot come forward and
say "I object" is a bad day for America.*
—Lindsey Graham

"I'll read some of it for you," I announced from the podium, holding a photocopied page from a book that has been praised by the American Library Association (ALA), *New York Times*, *Parenting* magazine, and *Bulletin of the Center for Children's Books*. I was there to speak to the Asheville, North Carolina, school board as a concerned citizen.

Across the cover of *It's Perfectly Normal*, the publisher boasts of selling more than a million copies to date. The introductory material includes praise from so-called experts in pediatrics and childhood development. So the book must be good, right?

"After a bit, a person's vagina becomes moist and slippery, and the clitoris becomes hard,"[1] I began, not deviating in the slightest from the text in front of me. With that one line, a school board member began talking over me, trying to get me to stop. But I continued: "After a bit, a person's penis becomes erect, stiff, and larger. Sometimes a bit of clear fluid that may contain a few sperm comes out of the tip of the penis and makes it wet."[2] The more I read, the more frantic and urgent the school board member's protests became.

Finally, I looked up from the paper and addressed the man who had been haranguing me for the last minute or so. "Was it something I said?" I asked.

Silence.

"If you don't want to hear it in a school board meeting, why should children be able to check it out of the school system?" I questioned, boldness now emanating from my gut. But I already knew the answer.

Filled with illustrations of naked people—old, young, handicapped, obese, black, and white—the book is pornographic. Sexual intercourse, including male-on-male and female-on-female, is depicted both in graphic text and through illustrations. A young boy is shown with his penis in his hand, masturbating on his bed. A girl is shown bending over, peering up between her legs to get a better look at her vagina. Oh—and the cover notes *It's Perfectly Normal* is for ages ten and up.

No matter what they tell you, this is not "perfectly normal."

Over the past several years, public schools and community libraries have become a battleground in the culture war. The amount of pornographic reading material being aimed at children in the name of inclusivity and LGBTQ+ rights is simply staggering. But most people don't know what their children have access to. Many assume that if the school board or library approved the reading material, it must be fine. But nothing could be further from the truth.

A while back, one of my more vocal critics nicknamed me "The Book-Banning Pastor" because as part of my ministry I visit school boards around the country and shed light on the perverted books being pushed on their students. My strategy is simple: I stand up, introduce myself, read a bit from one of the disgusting titles they allow elementary school children to check out from the school library, and wait for the response I always get: outrage. Of course, my goal is to have these local boards remove the filthy books from their schools and libraries, but I'm not a book banner; I'm simply against putting sexually suggestive and explicitly pornographic materials in the hands of kids.

I'm not the only person to point out the Left's hypocrisy on this issue. In the summer of 2023, Illinois passed a law that denies funding to libraries that allow books to be permanently removed—essentially silencing parents who object to the reading material that is available to their kids:

> House Bill 2789, sponsored by State Rep. Anne Stava-Murray (81st District—Downers Grove) and Sen. Laura Murphy (28th District—Elk Grove Village), allow[s] [Secretary of State] Giannoulias' office to authorize grant funding only to libraries that adhere to the American Library Association's Library Bill of Rights. The Bill of Rights states that reading materials should not be removed or restricted because of partisan or personal disapproval, or that issue a statement prohibiting the practice of banning books or resources.[3]

A short time later, U.S. Senator John Kennedy (a Republican from Louisiana) responded to this new statute that bans book banning, and in his remarks, read from two different books. Here's what he read from *All Boys Aren't Blue*:

I put some lube on and got him on his knees, and I began to slide into him from behind. I pulled out of him and kissed him while he masturbated. He asked me to turn over while he slipped a condom on himself. This was my ass, and I was struggling to imagine someone inside me. He got on top and slowly inserted himself into me. It was the worst pain I think I have ever felt in my life.[4]

And then it was time for a selection from *Gender Queer*:

I got a new strap-on harness today. I can't wait to put it on you. It will fit my favorite dildo perfectly. You're going to look so hot. I can't wait to have your cock in my mouth. I'm going to give you the blowjob of your life, then I want you inside of me.[5]

Mind you, these are books in school libraries—and this is the sort of utter filth the Illinois policymakers passed legislation to protect. Here's the spin Democrat governor J. B. Pritzker put on it:

Here in Illinois, we don't hide from the truth, we embrace it. . . . Young people shouldn't be kept from learning about the realities of our world; I want them to become critical thinkers, exposed to ideas that they disagree with, proud of what our nation has overcome.[6]

Uh-huh. This is all about helping kids develop critical-thinking skills. Right.

LGBTQ+ advocates and radical leftists want to frame this debate around the issue of banning books. After Kennedy's remarks, Illinois secretary of state Alexi Giannoulias compared *Gender Queer* to the modern literary classic *To Kill a*

Mockingbird, insisting that everyone should make up their own mind about what is appropriate and what is not.[7] But let's remember what we're really talking about:

> Sen. John Kennedy made waves on Tuesday after he read excerpts from the book *Gender Queer*, among others, during a hearing.
>
> The book in question is available in various public schools across the country and has become a symbol of the left's attempt to sexualize children. In light of that, parents across the political spectrum have risen up in order to reassert their rights and demand the removal of pornographic materials from classrooms.
>
> Astonishingly, Democrats have doubled down, proclaiming that Republicans are instituting "book bans" by passing laws to stop school libraries from stocking sexual content. Some states, such as Illinois, have even gone so far as to pass laws *against* the removal of pornographic materials from classrooms and libraries.[8]

U.S. Senator Dick Durbin, a Democrat from Illinois, responded to Kennedy's actions, saying, "Let's be clear, efforts to ban books are wrong, whether they come from the right or the left. . . . In the name of protecting students, we're instead denying these students an opportunity to learn about different people and difficult subjects."[9]

In a sense, Durbin and other Democrats are correct: This *is* about denying students the "opportunity to learn about different people and difficult subjects." But the "different people" are those who seek to sexualize and groom our children for exploitation and set them up for deeply rooted (and often life-long) physical, mental, emotional, and spiritual problems, and the "difficult subjects" are LGBTQ+ propaganda, pornographic literature, and instruction manuals for sexual deviancy.

☞

IN 2021, THE American Library Association Office for Intellectual Freedom tracked 1,597 books whose content had raised red flags for parents or concerned citizens. That's hard for me to wrap my mind around: Nearly sixteen hundred books were identified as being problematic.

While not every book was targeted because of sexual content or LGBTQ+ messaging, eight of the ten most frequently cited ones were. This is not some fringe issue related to a couple of titles from niche publishers; it reveals an ongoing assault on childhood and a movement to undermine parents across this nation. When I stand up at a school board meeting anywhere in the United States, I do so for one reason: to protect children. This shouldn't be controversial, and yet it is. Consider the following:

> On October 3rd, 2022, Rasmussen Reports published a nationwide poll with the commentary, "Voters overwhelmingly oppose sexually explicit books in public school libraries. . . . Sixty-nine percent (69%) of voters believe books containing explicit sexual depictions of sex acts. . . . should not be present in public high school libraries."
> One day later, on October 4th, Deseret News published a poll that they had conducted with a social media post declaring that "just 12% of Americans agree that books should be removed from libraries if a parent objects."[10]

At first, it might seem as though Americans don't know what they want. It seems they want to remove sexually explicit materials from public school libraries while also making sure no book is ever banned. But actually, when we dig deeper, we find that the way these surveys were conducted tells a deeper story:

> The Deseret News poll asked respondents if they agree with the following statement: *"If any parent objects to a book in the public school library, that book should be removed, even if other parents like the book."* Some may consider that question leading or possibly neglectful of the issue of sexually explicit materials, but I'll be gracious and just call it vague. . . .
>
> In contrast, the Rasmussen poll is very specific. It does not ask about just any parent or any book. The survey asks, *"Should books containing explicit sexual depictions of sex acts be present in public high school libraries?"* It makes perfect sense that respondents would respond to this question much differently than the broader query.[11]

This is why, when I stand up at school board meetings, I am cheered on by parents and average citizens alike. They understand the only way to expose the darkness is to bring the light—and that's what I do. By reading selections from the filth schools and sexual activists are serving our students, the pornographic content is revealed for what it is.

On the other hand, outside the building, I am sometimes met by protestors and LGBTQ+ activists. They yell all kinds of things at me, but usually their rancor has to do with me allegedly opposing the First Amendment, hating LGBTQ+ people, or wanting to ban books I disagree with. I get the same treatment on social media. If you can get people to think this debate is about free speech or suppressing dissenting viewpoints, you can gain a lot of sympathy for your agenda. But when it becomes evident it's really about keeping kids from some book-fair-approved version of *Hustler* magazine, most people stop screaming at me. As we've seen over and over again throughout this book, great confusion is created through the manipulation of language. The Left knows this, and they've become masters at controlling the mic, editing the dictionary, and hiding the truth.

Take, for example, the 2011 novel *Thirteen Reasons*. It's labeled as young adult fiction, and the ALA even named it one of the Best Books for Young Adults that year. Books for "young adults" are intended for (and marketed to) children ages twelve through eighteen.[12] So, if a book carries a "YA" label, parents should be able to give it to their twelve-year-old without worrying they've just handed him or her pornographic literature.

Here is an excerpt from that book. You can decide for yourself if you think this is appropriate material for an eighteen-year-old, let alone a twelve-year-old.

So congratulations, Bryce. You're the one. I let my reputation catch up with me—I let my reputation become me—with you. How does it feel?

Wait, don't answer that. Let me say this first: I was not attracted to you, Bryce. Ever. In fact, you disgusted me.

And I'm going to kick your ass. I swear it.

You were touching me . . . but I was using you. I needed you, so I could let go of me, completely.

For everyone listening, let me be clear. I did not say no or push his hand away. All I did was turn my head, clench my teeth, and fight back tears. And he saw that. He even told me to relax.

"Just relax," he said. "Everything will be okay." As if letting him finger me was going to cure all my problems.

But in the end, I never told you to get away . . . and you didn't.

You stopped rubbing circles on my stomach. Instead, you rubbed back and forth, gently; along my waist. Your pinky made

*its way under the top of my panties and rolled back and forth,
from hip to hip. Then another finger slipped below, pushing your
pinky further down, brushing it through my hair.*

*And that's all you needed, Bryce. You started kissing my
shoulder, my neck, sliding your fingers in and out. And then you
kept going. You didn't stop there.*

*I'm sorry. Is this getting too graphic for some of you? Too
bad.*[13]

Or take this one: *Flamer* by Mike Curato. Again, this is
labeled YA, and it's also a graphic novel, meaning it's a glorified comic book. On the cover, an endorsement from another
author, Jarrett J. Krosoczka, says, "This book will save lives."
Seems really important, right? Maybe even the sort of book
a parent would want to read alongside their child to foster
meaningful conversations about life. Here are a few high-
lights of this oh-so-important piece of trash—er, literature:

"Hey, Navarro, suck any good dicks lately? Hahahahaha!"[14]

"What's wrong, Navarro? I thought you like a big sau-
sage in your mouth! Haha!"[15]

(The illustration on the middle of the page depicts a young
teenage boy with a hotdog on a stick balanced between his
legs. Three other boys are watching him, laughing.)

A teenager standing up with the hotdog on a stick says,
"Okay, who wants my hot wiener?"

The other boy is saying, "Oh, yeah, baby, slide it right
into my buns."[16]

I learned about masturbation two years ago. Kind of by
accident. Nobody ever told me what it was. One day when
everyone was out of the house, I came across a video tape

hidden behind the TV. My dad had hidden movies before with dirty scenes, like *Fatal Attraction*. It was exciting to see boobs and butts. But this time, it was different. I could see . . . everything. People were doing things that I didn't even know were possible, or even . . . allowed? "Why is there so much hair? Those dicks are so . . . BIG." [The illustration on this page depicts the main character facing a small TV set with a remote control in his hand.][17]

Part of me wants to simply tell you there are filthy books being pushed on young children and leave it at that—no descriptions, no excerpts. I don't enjoy quoting sexually explicit material or putting it out there for more people to read. But this chapter is another way to shed light on what is happening in public schools all across our land. Sadly, most people don't have any idea about that. They just assume the teachers, administrators, and school board members in their community are their allies, that they're looking out for their children's best interests. But things are not so simple.

In 2020, when the COVID-19 pandemic shut down in-person instruction and had students learning from home, many parents got their first careful look at the curricula their sons and daughters were using. If you recall, that's when out-rage over Critical Race Theory and pro-LGBTQ+ content erupted. In fact, it was during that season that I first attended a school board meeting as a concerned parent.

As a youth pastor, I'm concerned about my students. How I wish they were all homeschooled or attended a Christian school! But that's not the case. Roughly 75 percent of students in North Carolina attend a public school, so it is our responsibility as Christians to make sure those schools are as good as they can be, even if our own children have other educational opportunities. I fight for school choice. I vote for school choice. But it simply will not do to ignore the public school system while we advocate for educational freedom. Government schools are not ideal—in fact, they are a tool of the radical left—but we cannot abdicate our responsibility to protect the innocent children forced to attend them.

During the pandemic, our lieutenant governor at the time, Mark Robinson, held a press conference to address the growing problem of books and curricula that were out of touch with the values of most parents in our state. He vowed to clean up the situation, and he certainly did his part. Mark's passion for the welfare of our kids was evident to me. After that, I felt the Lord prompting me to do something. I'm not a lieutenant governor, of course, so I knew I couldn't do anything through the power of the state. But I could stand up for kids. So that's what I did.

The first time I appeared before a school board, it was to speak out against a teacher who was stepping on the rights of a Christian student. The student in question had done a project on the Bible, but her atheist teacher demeaned her and told her talking to God was like talking to a wall. As I thought about what I would say before that school board, I reflected on the fact that there was a time, not too long ago, when the Bible was welcome in our public schools. Back then, there wasn't an epidemic of school shootings, and the academic performance of our nation's students was better across the board. Back then, we didn't teach kids math or reading through the lens of Critical Race Theory, homosexual behavior was not trumpeted as a badge of honor, and transgenderism was not even on our radar. As I stood before parents, teachers, and school board members, I declared, "Critical Race Theory will never solve racism, because it is racism."

I told the cheering crowd, "I'm against white supremacy, and I'm against black supremacy, but I'm for God's supremacy!"

I believe that sincerely. Many of the problems we're seeing today are the result of removing God from the public square. I can't help but think we wouldn't need to talk about problematic books like *It's Perfectly Normal* and *Flamer* if we still had the Bible in our schools. But we live in a world where the truth of God's Word has been exiled from public discussion in general, so people like me must stand up and bring the truth instead.

After that Chatham County school board meeting, I began stepping up to the mic at other school board meetings to speak not just about Critical Race Theory, but also the sexualization of our children. That's how I earned a reputation as the pastor who reads dirty books in public. But again, if these passages are appropriate for children, as my critics contend, they shouldn't object to them being read aloud to adults.

At a school board meeting in Florida in 2023, I read the same portion of *Thirteen Reasons Why* that I referenced earlier in this chapter. Before I could finish the first line, a school board member began shouting for me to stop. I kept right on reading. Within seconds, she ordered my mic to be cut off. I kept on reading—a bit louder to compensate for the loss of the mic. Before my allotted time was complete, three policemen had approached me and began pulling me away from the microphone. They escorted me from the building against my will—all for reading from a book that was freely available to kids through their local middle school and high school libraries.[18]

In Nevada, I read from *Flamer*, and once again a school board member began shouting over me. I suppose all the cussing, sexual language, and homoerotic imagery were too much for her sensibilities. She then insisted that my time was over. I informed her, "You don't have the authority to stop my time." That's when, once again, police stepped in to pull me from the podium and remove me from the building. (This time, there were four cops.) As I walked the aisle to the back door with my police escort, I could hear the parents there that day begin chanting, "Remove her!"—meaning the school board member.[19] They understood the problem is not people like me reading from pornographic books at school board meetings; it's people like that esteemed school board member, who would rather have our children reading that filth than listen to it herself.

In October 2023, I set my sights on the Cherry Creek School District, a Denver suburb in Colorado. State law expressly states that only local residents can speak at school board meetings. So I did what anyone would do: I leased an apartment in the area. And with my lease agreement in hand, I caught a flight to Colorado and prepared to read from a por-nographic book currently available in the district's school libraries. But a few hours before the meeting, I received an email telling me the board had decided not to permit me to have my two minutes on the floor. I responded and explained I was a legal resident in the district. But there was no further discussion; they simply told me the decision was final.

The more I attend school board meetings, doing nothing more than reading the filth these districts are providing to— and in some cases pushing upon—our children, the more resistance I face. I'm not surprised, though. As I mentioned in a previous chapter, it is in our sinful nature to want to silence anyone who offends us. But when you stand in truth, there's no reason to shut up. It is the truth—and only the truth—that will change the world for the better.

☞

LET'S BE CLEAR about what these books are doing to children: They are robbing them of their innocence. When we invite children into sexual encounters, even if only through the pages of a book or magazine, we are robbing them of their purity. You can never unsee pornographic images, and you can never unread salacious paragraphs.

When Jesus walked the earth, He welcomed children, took them up in His arms, and even held them high as an example we should follow, saying, "The kingdom of heaven belongs to such as these" (Matthew 19:14). He also issued a warning to the world:

If anyone causes one of these little ones—those who believe in me—to stumble, it would be better for them to have a large millstone hung around their neck and to be drowned in the depths of the sea. (Matthew 18:6)

A millstone was a large stone wheel that was hitched to a donkey; as the donkey walked around his enclosure, the wheel would turn to grind wheat. It was big and heavy. If one was hung around your neck and you were somehow tossed into the sea—a feat that would be nearly impossible because of the weight of the millstone—you would be done for. This is strong language from our Lord and Savior. He's not messing around. Jesus is a fierce defender of children. He was then, and He is now. He does not take kindly to those who seek to harm kids. And neither should we.

If radical leftists want to call me The Book-Banning Pastor, so be it. I'll wear the title proudly. I will not back down. My silence on the subject of pornographic books being foisted on children would make me complicit. It doesn't matter how many times they cut my mic, escort me out of the building, or arrest me (though it hasn't come to that—yet). As the Apostle Paul wrote, "Let God be true, and every human being a liar" (Romans 3:4).

CHAPTER 9

LIE #9: THE BIBLE ISN'T POLITICAL, SO CHRISTIANS SHOULD STAY OUT OF POLITICS

What are kingdoms without justice?
They're just gangs of bandits.
—Augustine

During the American Revolution, pastors throughout the
thirteen colonies overwhelmingly supported independence and the military effort to defeat the British. It is believed
that without their fiery preaching, the Continental Army and
its militias would not have had what it took to stand against
the Redcoats long enough to win the war. These pastors of
conviction were so influential that the British dubbed them
"The Black-Robed Regiment."[1]

Oh, how far we've fallen!

Today, pastors and Christian leaders seem to go out of their way to avoid being political, especially on the Right. Many say they don't want to alienate unbelievers who might be turned away by political talk. It's for the sake of the Gospel, they tell us. Others don't want to talk about current events or hot-button issues because they may divide the congregation. So for the sake of unity, they feel they must avoid mentioning abortion, CRT, and transgenderism in their sermons.

But there are some who try to tell us that the reason they're not political is because Jesus wasn't political, and for that matter, neither is the Bible.

Nothing could be further from the truth.

Let's start with Jesus. You may have heard that Jesus wasn't political because He didn't overthrow the Romans or even speak out against Caesar. But He didn't have to. His entire ministry was centered on a new Kingdom, one over which He would rule:

> After John was put in prison, Jesus went into Galilee, proclaiming the good news of God. "The time has come," he said. "The kingdom of God has come near. Repent and believe the good news!" (Mark 1:14–15)

What could be more political than bringing your own kingdom to the earth? It's true Jesus wasn't some '60s-styled hippie, protesting foreign wars in the streets of Jerusalem. Nor was He a lobbyist to the Sanhedrin, mixing it up with the who's who of the religious establishment to move His agenda forward. Jesus's political engagement looked nothing like the sorts of things we see today. Even so, He was incredibly political.

He challenged the religious establishment, sometimes through direct confrontation—like when He tossed over the tables of the money changers in the Temple's Court of the Gentiles (see John 2:13–25)—but more often through His subversive teaching style: "You have heard that it was said . . ." (Matthew 5:21, 27, 33, 38, 43). Jesus was not contradicting the Old Testament Law, but rather the Pharisees' interpretation and application of it. In doing so, He revealed His Father's heart and will, and declared the religious gatekeepers to be out of step with Heaven.

When it came to Rome, Jesus was even more subversive. The Lord famously told His followers, "If anyone forces you to go one mile, go with them two miles" (5:41). Today, we hear these words as a call to give everything we've got. It's part of the Puritan work ethic to go the extra mile. But that's not what Jesus was saying, nor what His original hearers would have understood. In the first century, Judea and Galilee were provinces of the Roman Empire, and their Jewish residents were little more than slaves. Roman law permitted soldiers to force a non-citizen to carry their gear up to one mile.

By telling His followers to "go with them two miles," Jesus was inverting the master/slave dynamic. The first mile was forced, but the second mile would be a choice. It was a way of saying, "This is a gift." It was a way of declaring true freedom—of a kind even the Romans couldn't quash. Only the cruelest of soldiers would lash out at the free mile of service; most would realize that they now owed a debt of thanks to a man whom, just two miles earlier, they would have considered about as valuable as a pack mule. This is the sort of move that shifts power, that reveals the true nature of the world.

When He appeared before Pilate, bloodied and beaten from a scourging, the Son of God calmly stated the facts: "You would have no power over me if it were not given to you from above. Therefore the one who handed me over to you is guilty of a greater sin" (John 19:11). That right there is a political statement—"My Father is the true King of this world. You're only standing where you are because He permits it."

Even Jesus's birth is steeped in political drama. I know—when we think about the manger and shepherds and angels and Bethlehem, we don't ordinarily think *political intrigue*. But let's frame the story in its historical context:

> It made perfect sense that Jesus would choose to come as one of those underdogs of a political Empire—a vulnerable child with nowhere to go, his parents shuffled about by the Roman demand for a census.
>
> But here's what we miss about Jesus' birth. There are really only two goals in carrying out a major census—the kind that framed his entry into the world. Just two reasons to go to all that extra expense and bureaucratic hassle to count every single head in the entire Roman world (Lk 2:1).
>
> The first reason is to determine **the number of people who can pay taxes.**
>
> And the second is to figure out **the number of men who can fight in an army.**
>
> Tax and War. Money and Power. Politics.
>
> In other words, the birth of Christ took place in the shadow of the twin pillars of a typical political Empire: economic power and military might.[2]

And of course, there was the angel's announcement to the shepherds:

> But the angel said to them, "Do not be afraid. I bring you good news that will cause great joy for all the people. Today in the town of David a Savior has been born to you; he is the Messiah, the Lord." (Luke 2:10–11)

We're so accustomed to hearing this during every Christmas Eve service and every rewatching of *A Charlie Brown Christmas* that we miss the political aspect of Jesus's birth. Back in the first century the "good news" or the "gospel" was about Caesar:

> An inscription published in the year 9 BC for a calendar reform of the cities of Asia Minor in the town of Priene speaks the language of the imperial cult: there, the birth of Emperor Augustus, the "Son of God," is a "birth of God," bringing the "Saviour" and creating "peace"—the beginning—literally in Greek—of all the "Gospels." With the birthday of the emperor, the new calendar is to begin.
>
> On this "Calendar Inscription of Priene," which came to the Collection of Classical Antiquities in Berlin from an excavation in 1899, the proximity between the biblical narrative of the birth of Christ and the imperial cult is palpable. The New Testament writings reinterpret all this: The Christ-birth trumps the emperor, the holy gospel is quite different from the imperial "gospel" of bloody victory-peace with which the Roman emperors subjugated the world.[3]

Jesus's entrance into our world was a political statement like no other. And the Church, from the very beginning, understood this. When the Gospel writers sat down to pen their accounts, they made sure the political undertones remained.

Rather than being the apolitical Mr. Rogers in sandals many people imagine He was, Jesus saw all of life through His Father's eyes, including politics, power, and position. And this is what we should expect from the Son of God. The entire Bible is an inherently political document. Through and through, it is a collection of documents designed to upend the status quo of sinful human power structures.

Genesis opens with God creating a good world. In doing so, He establishes Himself as the King and ultimate Authority over the universe. But as soon as God forms human beings in His image, He gives them dominion—that is, government—of His creation:

> God blessed them and said to them, "Be fruitful and increase in number; fill the earth and subdue it. Rule over the fish in the sea and the birds in the sky and over every living creature that moves on the ground." (Genesis 1:28)

This is the birth of politics. God put humanity in charge of the world, but the question is: How will we rule? Every political debate is really about answering that foundational issue. And across the centuries, there have been many, many attempts to answer it—so many, in fact, that we have often forgotten the purpose of our rule: to bear God's image to one another (see Genesis 1:26–27). In other words, we are supposed to govern in a way that reveals God's good heart.

In Scripture, church is the *ekklesia*—a Greek word meaning "a regularly summoned legislative body, *assembly*."[4] It comes from the Greek root *kaleo*, meaning "to call." The Church is the community of the called-out ones. We have actually been given the assignment of legislating things on Earth to line up with God's original intent—to make things here like they are in Heaven. What could be more "political" than being a legislative body? Much of the Old Testament centers on the various kings of Israel and Judah, and how their governments affected the people in their care. Good kings led the people toward Yahweh and the blessings that flow from living according to His ways. Evil kings led the people toward false gods and idolatry, and they found themselves in bondage to darkness. Eventually, they were exiled.

Prophets spoke to power, both in the Holy Land and in the empires of the world. Joseph advised a pharaoh of Egypt; Moses confronted another one. Daniel held a high position in Babylon and continued influencing kings after Babylon was conquered by the Medes and the Persians. Esther used her beauty and the position it garnered her to save the Jewish people from genocide by appealing to her husband, King Xerxes of Persia. Nehemiah served as the cupbearer to King Artaxerxes and, because he had proven himself trustworthy, was given a commission to govern Judah and rebuild Jerusalem's walls. This is just a sampling from some of the major movements of the Old Testament. In the New, things get far more serious.

As Jesus's followers, we are caught between two kingdoms—the Kingdom of God and whatever kingdom in which we reside here on earth. We have become "a chosen people, a royal priesthood, a holy nation, God's special possession, that you may declare the praises of him who called you out of darkness into his wonderful light" (1 Peter 2:9). As a "royal priesthood," we have been called to be kings and priests unto God. He has renewed the commission He gave to Adam and Eve back in the Garden. What's more—the Lord has made us "Christ's ambassadors, as though God were making his appeal through us. We implore you on Christ's behalf: Be reconciled to God" (2 Corinthians 5:20).

Many people assume this ambassadorship is just a metaphor. "Our real work is mere evangelism and not political in any real sense," they tell us. But what could be more political than representing another kingdom here on Earth?

Of course, our ambassadorship *is* for the purpose of evangelism, but what does evangelism do? It transfers people from one kingdom to another:

For he has rescued us from the dominion of darkness and brought us into the kingdom of the Son he loves, in whom we have redemption, the forgiveness of sins. (Colossians 1:13–14)

This is part of the story of redemption. It's the clash of two kingdoms. It's a political battle that takes place in the heavenly realm *and* here on Earth. Notice that when Jesus commissioned His disciples after His resurrection, He said,

"Therefore go and make disciples of all nations, baptizing them in the name of the Father and of the Son and of the Holy Spirit, and teaching them to obey everything I have commanded you." (Matthew 28:19–20)

He didn't say we are to "make disciples of all people," though of course it's implied the Gospel message is for individuals. But His emphasis was on transforming nations. It's territorial, geographic, and political. That's why, at the end of the story, in the Book of Revelation, an angel blasts his trumpet and loud voices from Heaven declare, "The kingdom of the world has become the kingdom of our Lord and of his Messiah, and he will reign for ever and ever" (Revelation 11:15). That was always the goal—to make the whole world part of God's Kingdom, and in the end, God will bring it to completion. The question for us is, and always has been, what's our part?

☞

MANY BELIEVERS WILL want to stop me right here. They'll smile, pull out their Bible, and flip through the pages until they reach Romans 13:

Let everyone be subject to the governing authorities, for there is no authority except that which God has established. The authorities that exist have been established by God. Consequently, whoever rebels against the authority is rebelling against what God has instituted, and those who do so will bring judgment on themselves. (Romans 13:1–2)

Checkmate.

Pulled from its original context, this sure does sound like we are not to engage in politics whatsoever. No protesting, no complaining, no trying to change anything. We probably shouldn't even vote. God has everyone in place, just where He wants them. Who are we to seek a new president or congressman?

And then there's Jesus Himself. After all, He did say, "Give back to Caesar what is Caesar's" (Mark 12:17). That sure sounds like we should just be quiet, obey the government, and mind our own business.

Let's deal with Romans 13:1–2 first. Paul has just finished telling Roman believers not to repay anyone evil for evil (12:17). Vengeance is a natural impulse when persecution comes our way. But Paul says, "Do not be overcome by evil, but overcome evil with good" (v. 21). That is why He says we should be subject to the governing authorities. If we become men and women who commit crimes against those who hurt us, we will be no better than our persecutors—and we will have lost our witness for Christ. Paul is not saying Christians should keep out of politics—or even that we should blindly follow every edict and mandate issued by our elected officials and representatives.

So how do we know when we should disobey or when we should speak out against our own government? We'll come back to that. First, let's unpack what Jesus was saying about giving back to Caesar. To do that, we'll need to review the full context:

> Later they sent some of the Pharisees and Herodians to Jesus to catch him in his words. They came to him and said, "Teacher, we know that you are a man of integrity. You aren't swayed by others, because you pay no attention to who they are; but you teach the way of God in accordance with the truth. Is it right to pay the imperial tax to Caesar or not? Should we pay or shouldn't we?"
>
> But Jesus knew their hypocrisy. "Why are you trying to trap me?" he asked. "Bring me a denarius and let me look at it." They brought the coin, and he asked them, "Whose image is this? And whose inscription?"
>
> "Caesar's," they replied.
>
> Then Jesus said to them, "Give back to Caesar what is Caesar's and to God what is God's."
>
> And they were amazed at him. (Mark 12:13–17)

They were trying to trap Jesus. By asking Him about paying taxes, they thought they had Him cornered. If He said yes, the people should pay taxes to Rome, He would be affirming the Roman Empire's right to rule over God's people—something the crowds would despise Him for saying. And if He said no, the people should not pay their taxes, the Pharisees and Herodians could report Him to the Roman authorities for sedition.

Jesus is brilliant; how He responded changed the game. The coin used to pay the tax had Caesar's image on it. Therefore, it belonged to him. Jesus affirmed the people should pay their taxes, but He did so without praising or affirming Rome. You and me, though? We bear *God's* image. That means we belong

to Him. And as Jesus says, we are to "give . . . to God what is
God's" (v. 17). That means our whole lives. For the sake of our
discussion in this chapter, that includes our politics.

But all this brings us back to the question of how we know
when to speak up, stand up, and resist governmental authorities. Acts 5 gives us the example of the apostles:

> The apostles performed many signs and wonders among
> the people. . . . As a result, people brought the sick into
> the streets and laid them on beds and mats so that at least
> Peter's shadow might fall on some of them as he passed by.
> Crowds gathered also from the towns around Jerusalem,
> bringing their sick and those tormented by impure spirits,
> and all of them were healed. (Acts 5:12, 15–16)

The Jewish leaders responded to this display of God's
power by arresting the apostles and putting them in jail. "But
during the night an angel of the Lord opened the doors of the
jail and brought them out" (v. 19). Undeterred, the high priest
and his cabal had the apostles arrested once more. Here's
what happened:

> The apostles were brought in and made to appear before
> the Sanhedrin to be questioned by the high priest. "We
> gave you strict orders not to teach in this name," he said.
> "Yet you have filled Jerusalem with your teaching and are
> determined to make us guilty of this man's blood."
> Peter and the other apostles replied: "We must obey God
> rather than human beings! The God of our ancestors raised
> Jesus from the dead—whom you killed by hanging him on
> a cross. God exalted him to his own right hand as Prince
> and Savior that he might bring Israel to repentance and
> forgive their sins. We are witnesses of these things, and so

is the Holy Spirit, whom God has given to those who obey him." (Acts 5:27–32)

The apostles understood the proper spheres of authority. The Sanhedrin certainly had some measure of authority in Jerusalem, and the Romans had jurisdiction over their empire. But God was still the King of the Universe—and Jesus had been "exalted . . . to his own right hand as Prince and Savior" (v. 31). God's commands always supersede the commands of men. Our citizenship in the Kingdom of Heaven always exceeds our citizenship here on Earth. "We must obey God rather than human beings!" (v. 29).

☞

I REALIZE THAT, to many, the idea that Christians should be involved in politics is a terrifying notion. Images of a theocratic state—something out of *A Handmaid's Tale*—come to life. These well-meaning believers fear that power in the hands of the Church will lead to a distortion of the Gospel and a lust for power that will render Jesus's teachings inert.

These objections are not without warrant, as history shows the meshing of church and civil government can have disastrous results. However, Christian political engagement does not mean pushing for a state church or a regime run by religious zealots. Rather, it means that Christians in every society and at every level of society are to follow Jesus above all earthly powers and, when necessary, speak prophetically to those in authority.

Theologian Wayne Grudem argues that engaging in politics is part of God's command for us to steward creation and bless others:

One reason why Jesus left us here on earth is that we should glorify him *by doing good to other people in all areas of life.* "So then, as we have opportunity, let us do good to everyone, and especially to those who are of the household of faith" (Gal. 6:10 [ESV]). Certainly that means that we should do good to others, as we have opportunity, by being a good influence on laws and government and by having a good influence on the political process. . . .

Jesus left us here on earth in part because he wants to allow our lives to give glory to him in the midst of a fallen and sinful world: "Let your light shine before others, *so that they may see your good works* and give glory to your Father who is in heaven" (Matt. 5:16 [ESV]).

So, should churches teach their people how to do "good works" in hospitals and in schools, and in businesses and in neighborhoods, but not in government? Why should that area of life be excluded from the influence of the "good works" of believers that will "give glory to your Father who is in heaven"?

I conclude that Jesus' command that "you shall love your neighbor as yourself" [Matthew 22:39 ESV] means that I should seek the good of my neighbors in every aspect of society, *including seeking to bring about good government and good laws.*[5]

You can almost hear in Grudem's comments an echo of God's command in Jeremiah 29:7, which says, "Seek the peace and prosperity of the city to which I have carried you into exile. Pray to the Lord for it, because if it prospers, you too will prosper." Our allegiance is first and foremost to the Kingdom of God, but while we're exiles here in this world, we need to seek the peace and prosperity of our communities, doing good to everyone. That means our political voices should be used to promote human flourishing.

Another objection to Christian engagement in politics is that it can be used to gain power. But that is like saying Christians shouldn't be involved in eating because it will involve chewing. Of course political engagement is about wielding power; that's what politics is. Political power, in and of itself, is not a bad thing; it's what we do with that power that matters.

When I go to a school board meeting and confront members with the filthy books they have allowed in their districts' libraries, some people say I'm being unnecessarily crass. Others say I'm being provocative to draw attention to myself. There are even those who say I'm being unloving to my LGBTQ+ neighbors. But the truth is, I'm caring for children by calling attention to material that seeks to destroy their innocence and groom them into a lifestyle that will ultimately destroy them. It all comes down to one simple question: Is our society better without those books in the hands of young people? I think it is.

When I draw attention to the lies of Critical Race Theory and diversity programs, some call me a racist—I've even been called a white supremacist!—but the truth is, it's because I love people of color so much that I can't stand to see them being deceived and manipulated. Being told that every problem in your life is the result of someone else's bigotry feeds resentment, destroys hope, and sows division— and it's simply not true. DEI initiatives will never heal our nation or our communities. I proudly stand against it in my desire to bless others.

And when I stand outside abortion clinics with other believers, praying for the women inside to change their minds, it's not because I hate women, as some have charged. It's not because I've taken up a "white man's issue," as others have said. It's because I love God and all those made in His image, including those tiny babies still growing inside their mothers' wombs. And I love those mothers. I've met too many women who have had abortions they later regretted. They live with an ache that only Jesus can heal because they know they have murdered their own child. As I speak out against the evils of abortion, I hope to spare them the pain I know will come if they proceed with their plans.

These days, it seems it's only acceptable to be a politically minded Christian if you swing to the Left. In 2019, a former editor in chief of the so-called "evangelical flagship magazine" *Christianity Today*[6] famously called on evangelicals to abandon their support for President Donald Trump, saying:

> To use an old cliché, it's time to call a spade a spade, to say that no matter how many hands we win in this political poker game, we are playing with a stacked deck of gross immorality and ethical incompetence. Just when we think it's time to push all our chips to the center of the table, that's when the whole game will come crashing down. It will crash down on the reputation of evangelical religion and on the world's understanding of the gospel. And it will come crashing down on a nation of men and women whose welfare is also our concern.[7]

On the surface, that sounds reasonable. Few conservatives will suggest that Donald Trump has led a squeaky-clean life of holiness. He's a sinner—and a pretty accomplished one, if we are to believe news reports, rumors, and court records. But this editorial wasn't really about Trump's character, nor was the impeachment that prompted it.

In 2016, the Democratic presidential candidate was Hillary Clinton, and in 2020, it was Joe Biden. It's hard to think of two people with worse character or more scandals to their names. Plus, both land solidly in the camp that wants baby murder, LGBTQ+ hysteria, open-border insanity, and free speech stifled for those who disagree with their talking points. But *Christianity Today* hasn't run any pieces calling for Biden's ouster. And if the allegations about his influence peddling are true—which they very much appear to be—then Biden is not only a man of terrible character, but a traitor to our nation.

It shouldn't surprise us that the editors of *Christianity Today* are soft on Democrats and tough on Republicans, especially those of the MAGA variety. An investigation into *CT* staffers' campaign contributions between 2015 and 2022 revealed they made extensive donations to Democrats' campaigns and none to Republicans':

Between 2015 and 2022, nine Christianity Today employees made 73 political donations. All of them went to Democrats. This tally includes President and CEO Timothy Dalrymple, who gave $300 in two separate payments to failed Georgia Senate candidate Sarah Riggs Amico.

Amico's platform, which includes protecting abortion "without exception" and repealing the Hyde Amendment to allow federal tax dollars to fund abortions, contrasts sharply with the views of evangelicals who overwhelmingly say abortion should be illegal in all or most cases. She is also at odds with traditional Christian beliefs when it comes to gender, sexuality, and religious liberty. . . .

Between October 2019 and November 2020, news editor Daniel Silliman made eight donations to five different pro-abortion, pro-LGBTQ+ candidates, among them, Massachusetts Senator Elizabeth Warren's presidential campaign. In addition to possessing a perfect voting score from Planned Parenthood and NARAL, Warren supported shutting down crisis pregnancy centers across the country, and her platform included requiring schools to admit biological men into women's sports and single-sex spaces. She also pledged to allow a gender dysphoric nine-year-old to approve anyone she appointed as education secretary.[8]

Not only is *Christianity Today*—which was founded by none other than Billy Graham—supposed to be an evangelical publication, meaning there should be no question about which side of certain issues the journalists and editorial staff land on, but professional integrity requires them to be politically neutral in practice.

> The Society of Professional Journalists holds that editorial staff should never contribute to candidates or campaigns. For reporters covering politics, the SPJ goes even further, cautioning that "almost no political activity is OK." . . . Yet two editors at *Christianity Today* contributed to Democrat campaigns at the same time they were covering politics.[9]

The team at *Christianity Today* is hardly alone. Many Christian institutions, ministries, and colleges have gone woke, accepting progressive policy positions as the new Christian morality. As the Church in America grows more and more biblically illiterate, we shouldn't be surprised to find this shift taking place. A staff member at the *Christian Chronicle* makes the connection:

> Progressivism is attractive to formerly biblical Christians because it offers a sort of "halfway house" that allows them to remain largely religious and socially responsible, but relieves them from the responsibility of holding to what

they consider to be antiquated biblical teachings such as miracles, the authority of Scripture, sexual holiness or the sinfulness of humanity.[10]

In his book *The Christian Left*, pastor Lucas Miles writes,

In order for the Christian Left to garner a stronger foothold among the masses and effectively propagate theological and spiritual enmity within the mainstream church, it must do two things:

It must create animosity toward conservatives and traditionalists who hold to biblical ideas regarding social issues.

It must create a sense of moral superiority among an elite group of people.

These goals are often accomplished by the Left's use of spiritual-sounding language and references to its good deeds plagiarized from true believers and adopted by the Left.

See if you recognize these common lines of thought from the Christian Left:

1. Jesus accepts everyone.
2. Jesus would never get in the way of the love between two people.
3. Jesus was a refugee.
4. Jesus accepts foreigners and strangers.
5. God doesn't create walls that prevent us from coming to him.
6. People need to live their truth.
7. Some people are just born gay (or bi or transgender).
8. A real Christian accepts everyone.

By using arguments like this the Left has systematically hijacked Christian and conservative themes in order to validate the libertinism and moral erosion that the Left not only embraces but also desires to force en masse."

What Miles is describing is the hijacking of Christian political engagement. On the one hand, conservatives have been shamed into keeping silent on political issues through a lie—namely that neither the Bible nor Jesus is particularly political, and therefore Christians should stay out of politics. Then, with the other hand, they use a weakened, twisted version of biblical ethics to uphold any and every progressive agenda item.

If you're a Christian who favors open borders, it's because you love the alien and the widow—and because Jesus was a refugee.[12] But if you're a Christian who believes we should clamp down on illegal immigration, you are a racist xenophobe and nothing like Jesus. If you're a Christian who affirms same-sex relationships and transgenderism, you're accepting of others, just like Jesus. But if you're a Christian who rejects the LGBTQ+ agenda, you're no better than the Pharisees in Jesus's day who scoffed when He ate with tax collectors and sinners.

Do you see how it works?

Don't fall for the lie that the Bible isn't political. But also don't be tricked into thinking that its politics line up neatly with the Democrat Party's platform. While it's certainly true that Jesus is neither a card-carrying Republican nor a Democrat, He's not neutral on the issues, either. In the book that bears his name, Joshua, who led the nation of Israel after Moses died, is confronted by the angelic commander of the Lord's army:

Joshua went up to him and asked, "Are you for us or for our enemies?"

"Neither," he replied, "but as commander of the army of the Lord I have now come." Then Joshua fell facedown to the ground in reverence, and asked him, "What message does my Lord have for his servant?" (Joshua 5:13–14)

As believers, we should never assume God is on our side when it comes to politics. It is we who must be on His side. And that is why we must always allow Scripture to inform our politics and never the other way around.

But make no mistake: We must be political. That's part of our calling as God's people who are ambassadors to this world.

CHAPTER 10

LIE #10: THE CHURCH IS NOT ESSENTIAL

During the pandemic, we believed that
worship was worth the risk.
—Bishop Patrick Lane Wooden Sr.

As you probably remember, while the COVID-19 pandemic was raging, nonessential businesses were forcibly shut down through government mandates in various towns and cities across the country. Big-box stores like Walmart and Home Depot stayed open, while local restaurants and mom-and-pop shops were suddenly closed. (People need their plastic stuff from China and new hammers, I suppose.) Liquor stores were deemed essential,[1] and in some places, strip clubs were, too.[2] Meanwhile, in many places across the country and around the world, churches were marked nonessential and forced to shut their doors. Those that weren't shuttered completely were told to meet only in small groups, outdoors—and singing wasn't allowed.

When this happened, many pastors and Christian leaders saw an opportunity instead of a problem. Turning to social media, they leaned into people's ability to stream church services from home. Not only was this approach easier than hosting in-person services, it also allowed Sunday mornings to be produced. Worship sets could be recorded ahead of time, as could the message. In many instances, rather than standing behind the podium in an empty church building, preaching to a camera, pastors delivered their sermons from the comfort of home. Through the power of YouTube, some churches actually found their "attendance" was growing. For churches that had already spread across multiple campuses, going all in on online church seemed the next logical step. Why settle for three or four campuses around town when you can make every home in the world a potential campus?

Frank Barry, COO, CMO, and cofounder of a church technology company called Tithe.ly, interviewed pastor and church growth expert Larry Osborne of North Coast Church in San Diego during the pandemic. "Larry told me that prior to the COVID-19 pandemic, he would have described North Coast as a church with seven campuses that also offers online services," Barry later said. "But his team has had to shift. North Coast is now an online church that has seven physical locations."[3] In Osborne's mind, church can exist entirely online; the physical locations are just an added bonus. This is like Amazon focusing on Amazon.com while also building physical grocery stores and bookstores in various cities. The stores are just the icing on the cake that is the company's website.

But a church isn't a website or a streaming experience; it's a community.

We talk a good deal about having "online communities," but let's be honest—real community happens face to face, not from behind an avatar through likes and clicks. Don't misunderstand me—I'm grateful for the technology that allows churches to broadcast their services. It's a blessing to those who are sick or homebound, and it provides a unique window into the life of faith for the curious. But watching church on a television or a computer screen is simply not the same as being there in person and doing life with fellow believers. So let us do what the author of Hebrews said we ought: "And let us not neglect our meeting together, as some people do, but encourage one another, especially now that the day of his return is drawing near" (Hebrews 10:25 NLT).

In the midst of the pandemic, when fear of the unknown was gripping millions of Americans, our churches were no longer open for searching souls. But that didn't stop people from reaching out to God. A survey commissioned by McLaughlin & Associates found that one in five non-Christians had started reading the Bible during the pandemic, and a full 44 percent of Americans saw it and the ensuing financial crisis as a "wake-up call for us to turn back to faith in God" and "signs of coming judgment."[4] Where was the local church when so many were seeing the spiritual answers to our world's troubles? In many places, it was not gathering at all.

There were notable exceptions, of course. John MacArthur's Grace Community Church in Southern California famously defied state and county restrictions on indoor worship services, living out the ethic of Acts 5:29: "We must obey God rather than human beings!" In 2021, MacArthur was asked about online church. Here's what he said:

> "Zoom church is not Church. . . . It's not Church. It's watching TV. There's nothing about that that fulfills the biblical definition of coming together, stimulating one another to love and good works, coming together.

"The definition of a church is crystal clear in the New Testament. We see the picture of it. They came together the first day of the week. They worshiped the Lord, they prayed. . . . It was fellowship and it was the breaking of bread in the Lord's supper."

MacArthur stated that church involves "coming together" and that "it doesn't even function unless people" are "mutually using their spiritual gifts for one another."

"We are only the Church when we are together," he continued. "The Church is the Church when it corporately worships, when it corporately prays, when it corporately hears preaching of the Word of God."[5]

MacArthur was right, not only about the true nature of church as defined by the Bible but also about the Constitution. Our nation's Founding Fathers rightly saw that church was essential to life, and so they enshrined in the Bill of Rights this restriction on the government's power: "Congress shall make no law respecting an establishment of religion, or prohibiting the free exercise thereof."[6]

That didn't stop the state of California or Los Angeles County from taking legal action against Grace Community Church. MacArthur defied their mandates, and the governmental authorities sought to make an example of him.[7] However, after about a year of legal maneuvering, both the state and the county settled with Grace. Each paid $400,000 in legal fees to the church and dropped the suit. That's because, in a separate case also originating from Southern California, the Supreme Court of the United States recognized that COVID-19 restrictions imposed upon churches violated the free exercise of religion. MacArthur's opponents saw the writing on the wall and decided to give up.[8]

The media painted MacArthur as an agitator who refused to comply with the government's health safety protocols out of stubbornness and ego. But at the core, MacArthur's decision to stand up to tyranny was about obedience to God. When many other pastors simply complied and played nice—even announcing that the lockdowns were a way to love their neighbors—MacArthur stood firm.

In the midst of the pandemic, Pastor Jeremiah Johnson wrote in the Grace to You blog:

> During the lockdowns, many churchgoers have gotten into the habit of not going to church. I'll admit it was convenient—in those weeks when Grace Community Church was closed—to sleep in each Sunday, rolling out of bed and onto the couch in time to watch the livestreamed service. But I'm grateful it was only a matter of weeks, and that the pattern did not have time to become a habit.
>
> Others have been apart from their local church bodies for significantly longer, whether by force or by choice. I fear many—including some from my own congregation—have grown accustomed to livestream services and flat-screen pastors, without considering everything else they're missing by staying home. They don't realize—or perhaps, don't care—that they're forfeiting the primary means of accountability, discipleship, and discipline, along with the primary place to use and refine their spiritual gifts. They're denying themselves the best opportunities to serve and grow with other believers, and the encouragement and sharpening that we find only in the body of Christ. Ultimately, and most importantly, it's an issue of obedience.[9]

Beyond discipleship and accountability, attending church has other, less obvious benefits. In 2019, a study of six thousand adults in Ireland age fifty and over found that "individuals who regularly attend religious services have fewer depressive symptoms than those who consider religion important but who don't worship frequently."[10] In 2022, Gallup pollsters found a similar phenomenon:

> Americans who are religious, as measured by religious service attendance, are more likely to say they are personally satisfied than those who are not religious. The January Gallup data indicate that 92% of those who attend church services weekly are satisfied, compared with 82% of those who attend less than monthly. The difference is even more evident in terms of the percentage who report being *very* satisfied—67% of those who attend weekly are very satisfied with their personal life, compared with 48% among those who are infrequent attenders. Weekly religious service attenders are, in fact, more likely to say they are very satisfied than are those who make $100,000 or more in annual household income.[11]

We were designed for worship, service, and community—and we find all of these at church. Is it any wonder that people report greater happiness when they attend regularly? In our consumer society, it's easy to ask, "What's in it for me?" But church has never been a storefront filled with religious goods; it's an expression of God's Kingdom here on Earth. And in the Kingdom, things work a little differently. In 1 Corinthians, Paul describes the Church as a body:

> Just as a body, though one, has many parts, but all its many parts form one body, so it is with Christ. For we were all baptized by one Spirit so as to form one body—whether Jews or Gentiles, slave or free—and we were all given the

one Spirit to drink. Even so the body is not made up of one part but of many.

Now if the foot should say, "Because I am not a hand, I do not belong to the body," it would not for that reason stop being part of the body. And if the ear should say, "Because I am not an eye, I do not belong to the body," it would not for that reason stop being part of the body. If the whole body were an eye, where would the sense of hearing be? If the whole body were an ear, where would the sense of smell be? But in fact God has placed the parts in the body, every one of them, just as he wanted them to be. If they were all one part, where would the body be? As it is, there are many parts, but one body. . . .

Now you are the body of Christ, and each one of you is a part of it. (1 Corinthians 12:12–20, 27)

Just as it is with the various parts of the human body, we need each other. And watching church online or only attending when we need a spiritual pick-me-up just won't work. Church is essential for believers—and it's also essential for our society. To that subject we'll turn next.

☞

WHEN WE THINK about the civil rights movement of the 1960s, the image most of us conjure includes black churches rising up and peacefully but resolutely marching for change. But that's only half the story.

When the Civil Rights Act of 1866 became law, granting black Americans and former slaves full citizenship in the Union, it seemed that our nation would finally live up to its stated ideal that "all men are created equal." But over time, federal troops left the South and Democrats took over the government at the local and state levels. Before long, Jim Crow laws were enacted, and black people once again became second-class citizens, losing many of the rights guaranteed to them in the Constitution.

You might think that this would have sparked a revolution of sorts within black churches. But it didn't. Instead, many black ministers turned the focus of their churches inward. The churches themselves became shelters and sanctuaries for black Americans, but they were not the force for change we might have expected:

> They elected church leaders, pastors, trustees, deacons, and church boards. They remained the only independent institutions and became the only places in the South where talented African Americans could achieve some degree of success and respect. Sometimes they could even serve as liaisons with the white culture while not entering politics directly. . . . Generally however, Black churches in the South had to keep a low profile. Many reemphasized this part of evangelical tradition that stressed the inner relation with Christ and concentration on spiritual, otherworldly matters. This direction was additionally encouraged by the white landowners (even financially). Some previously active churches were simply silenced by threats of violence. . . . In this period of distress, many Black churches became a religious and psychological refuge for African Americans and served a therapeutic function.[12]

In 1957, the Reverend Dr. Martin Luther King Jr. founded the Southern Christian Leadership Conference. The organization offered training and resources to help black churches fight segregation in their local contexts. It was only through King's leadership that the Church really began to take on its prophetic role in our society. Some white Christians and white churches also stepped up, but it was the black churches that took the lead and became the core of the movement.

> They provided meeting places, information centers, and activists. Even if they were not directly recruiting volunteers, they provided information that shaped the political actions of congregants. . . . Being the best educated within Black communities and having some experience with leadership, Black preachers were qualified to play an active role in the CRM—and a number of them did.[13]

Of course, this chapter is about the Church generally, not just the black church in America. But I bring up this example because it shows just how important the Church is in the life of a society. We can see the stark contrast between what it looks like when the Church is inwardly focused and silent and the difference it makes when we take up our prophetic mantle as the people of God.

Jesus said His disciples are to be salt and light in the world (see Matthew 5:13–16). Salt is a preservative. As the Church speaks into the life of the communities and nation of which she is a part, it restrains some measure of evil. But when the Church is silent, there is no limit to the wickedness that will prevail.

Salt also was a form of currency in the ancient world. It was so valuable that people were sometimes paid in salt. (That's where we get the expression, "He isn't worth his salt.") Local churches should add value to their communities, blessing not only their own members but everyone in town.

Light shatters darkness. It shines so the truth can be seen clearly. In our world, there is a lot of confusion, too many voices adding to the noise. But the Church has the unique perspective of God's Word, and we should never be afraid to speak boldly. We can bring truth to bear when the lies seem overwhelming. This has happened time and again throughout history.

There was William Wilberforce the outspoken Christian and member of Parliament who fought to end Britain's slave trade. There was German pastor and theologian Dietrich Bonhoeffer, who resisted the Nazis when most of the Lutheran ministers in his country acquiesced to unspeakable evil. And there was the aforementioned Dr. Martin Luther King Jr., who spoke truth to power and led a nonviolent resistance movement against racial injustice. But the truth is, there are countless examples of the Church throughout history bringing salt and light to the world.

It's not just a prophetic voice the Church has to offer. When a natural disaster strikes, churches often open their doors to those in need before anyone else. It is the Church that sponsors and staffs local rescue missions to help the homeless. It is the Church that sets up crisis pregnancy centers to save the most vulnerable from abortion. But the most important thing the Church brings to the world is the Gospel.

I understand why men like Gavin Newsom and Anthony Fauci cannot understand why the Church would be essential during a time of unprecedented fear and anxiety—when the death toll was rising faster than the national debt. But the Gospel of Jesus Christ is the most important message a person can receive, and it was certainly needed when people were navigating a once-in-a-lifetime pandemic of biblical proportions.

Paul David Tripp, writing just as the COVID-19 lockdowns were setting in and we still had yet to learn just how disastrous the situation would become, reminds us of the Gospel's importance in uncertain times:

As this pandemic has spread from country to country until the entire globe is affected and is shutting down in an attempt to squash its power and its spread, we're reminded that there is an even greater, darker, more dangerous pandemic. It gets everyone—it gets everyone from birth. It is the deepest, darkest infection. It is the ultimate disease. It's called sin. It's more dangerous and more destructive than COVID-19 will ever be.

But this is what's amazing: there is a cure. God looked at his world in awesome mercy and love and decided he would not let us die from this disease. He sent his son to live as we could not live, to die an acceptable death, and to rise again—conquering sin and death so that there would be a cure for the ultimate disease. The cure is found in the person and work of the Lord Jesus, through his amazing grace. Celebrate grace. Celebrate that something more dangerous and more deadly than this pandemic will ever be has been cured by the power of the grace of Jesus. What a good thing.[14]

Jesus Christ is the hope of the world, and the Church has been commissioned to bring the gospel to every nation—and also to bring it to bear on every area of life. The Good News is not our religious perspective. It's not our preference. It's the truth. Jesus Christ is King of this world, and His Word is correct in every way. The sooner we, as the Church, begin living like we really believe this is true, the sooner we'll be able to make a sustained difference in this world.

☞

MATTHEW 16 DESCRIBES the time Jesus and His disciples traveled to the region of Caesarea Philippi, known as Bashan in the Old Testament period. It was a pagan center in their day, standing at the end of a long history of wickedness and idolatry. Bible scholar Michael Heiser explains:

> For the disciples, Bashan was an evil, otherworldly domain. But they had two other reasons to feel queasy about where they were standing. According to Jewish tradition, Mount Hermon was the location where the divine sons of God had descended from heaven—ultimately corrupting humankind via their offspring with human women (see Gen 6:1–4). These offspring were known as Nephilim, ancestors of the Anakim and the Rephaim (Num 13:30–33). In Jewish theology, the spirits of these giants were demons (1 Enoch 15:1–12).
>
> To make the region even spookier, Caesarea Philippi had been built and dedicated to Zeus. This pagan god was worshiped at a religious center built a short distance from the more ancient one in Dan—at the foot of Mount Hermon. Aside from the brief interlude during the time of Joshua through Solomon, the gates of hell were continually open for business.[15]

The gates of Hell, or Hades, was a real place. A cave dedicated to the god Pan, near the city of Caesarea Philippi, was believed to be the entrance to the realm of the dead, or the underworld. This was a dark, dark place—and yet Jesus chose to go there with His disciples.

It was in this setting that Peter made his good confession: "You are the Messiah, the Son of the living God" (Matthew 16:16). And then Jesus said something strange:

> Jesus replied, "Blessed are you, Simon son of Jonah, for this was not revealed to you by flesh and blood, but by my

Father in heaven. And I tell you that you are Peter, and on this rock I will build my church, and the gates of Hades will not overcome it." (Matthew 16:17–18)

This is the first of only two mentions of the "church"—the *ekklesia*—in the gospels. And it is here that Jesus tells us the Church's purpose: to storm the gates of Hell. I know—we've all been taught things about church, like it's a hospital for broken people, a place for worship, and even a place where people come to get right with God. It is all those things, but the Church is so much more than a place. It is a force for good in this world meant to take on the powers of darkness.

Have you ever noticed how Paul and the other apostles went out into a pagan world filled with demons and false gods, and within a few hundred years, all of the Roman Empire had been transformed? Just read through the Book of Acts, and you'll see temples to dark deities, demoniacs, and pagan gods galore. What happened to all of that? It's gone because the Church did its job so effectively, storming the gates of Hell. Though many people have been convinced the gospel is only about personal salvation, it actually transforms entire nations. That's the power of the Church—the power of the Holy Spirit at work in the lives of God's people.

Look around. It's clear America is in a dark place right now. Things are so bad, the situation can seem downright hopeless. The problems pile up so steeply that it's hard to see past them. But remember what Jesus said: "In this world you will have trouble. But take heart! I have overcome the world" (John 16:33).

Nothing is impossible for the Lord. And it just so happens, He has chosen to use His Church as His hands and feet in this world. That is why Paul, in closing his letter to the Romans, wrote, "The God of peace will soon crush Satan under your feet" (Romans 16:20). Did you catch what he did there? It was the Savior who was supposed to crush the head of the serpent (see Genesis 3:15). That's the way it was prophesied. But Paul knew that God works through His people. So, it is God who crushes Satan, but it will be through the Church's feet. That is how powerful the Church is in this world. And it is just one more reason why the Church will endure until the end of time—and will always be essential.

A POWERFUL DELUSION, OR A SHORT
BIBLE STUDY ON THE END TIMES

For this reason God sends them a powerful delusion so that they
will believe the lie and so that all will be condemned who have
not believed the truth but have delighted in wickedness.
—2 Thessalonians 2:11–12

No one knows for sure precisely when Jesus will return to Earth for His Bride, the Church. There is no shortage of prognosticators, would-be prophets, and self-proclaimed men of Issachar, who say they understand the times (see 1 Chronicles 12:32). But no one knows for sure. When He walked the earth, Jesus Himself said, "But about that day or hour no one knows, not even the angels in heaven, nor the Son, but only the Father" (Matthew 24:36). So, if someone tells you they know for sure, hold on to your wallet.

Even so, it's hard to deny the days are getting darker. Evil forces seem to be mustering in a unique way. There is an assault on children, reality is denied, death is celebrated, and the things of God are openly mocked. I recognize there have always been dark seasons. No one who lived through the Holocaust thought they were experiencing sunny days. No one who survived the Black Death said they were living their best life now. No Christian who was fed to lions in ancient Rome believed the Kingdom had appeared in its fullness. In fact, according to the New Testament, the end of days began with the death and resurrection of Christ. Writing to believers in Corinth in the middle of the first century, Paul described their generation as those "on whom the end of the ages has come" (1 Corinthians 10:11 ESV).

Whether or not Christ's return is just months away or a full millennium in the future, we must understand that we are living in the end times *right now*. That should affect how we live every day. We have a Savior coming, and the time is short! We must also understand what is going on in the world around us. There is no neutral ground; a war is being waged. Hear what Paul told the believers in Thessalonica who were worried they had missed Christ's return:

> For the secret power of lawlessness is already at work; but the one who now holds it back will continue to do so till he is taken out of the way. And then the lawless one will be revealed, whom the Lord Jesus will overthrow with the breath of his mouth and destroy by the splendor of his coming. The coming of the lawless one will be in accordance with how Satan works. He will use all sorts of displays of power through signs and wonders that serve the lie, and all the ways that wickedness deceives those who are perishing. They perish because they refused to love the truth and so be saved. For this reason God sends them a powerful delusion

so that they will believe the lie and so that all will be condemned who have not believed the truth but have delighted in wickedness. (2 Thessalonians 2:7–12)

Though Paul is talking specifically about delusions related to the revealing of the Antichrist, he is also describing the spirit of the age—"for the secret power of lawlessness is already at work" (v. 7). This is an age of lies and illusions, when people will be fooled into believing that which is not true. To put it another way, unbelievers, in large numbers, are being hoodwinked. Not only that, many who profess Christ are also being duped. If you see a rainbow flag outside a church building, that is no Christian church. If you see a group of believers marching with BLM,[1] you can be sure they've been deceived. And if you see pastors and church leaders offering you their pronouns, run the other way!

As it is in every age, there is a great temptation to be accepted by the culture at large. No one wants to be mocked or derided, persecuted or shamed. We all want the inside track to the good life. And so, that's where Satan tempts us. It starts out with a small compromise here or there—not saying anything when a brother puts his pronouns in his bio on social media. There's Marxist diversity training at the office, and Christians are silent for fear of losing their jobs. The weakest among us start losing our sensitivity to the lies, wanting to fit in and get along with others. "Isn't that what loving our neighbors looks like?" they ask. "You have a religious spirit, just like the Pharisees in Jesus's day," they say accusingly.

Here's how Paul explained it:

For the time will come when people will not put up with sound doctrine. Instead, to suit their own desires, they will

> gather around them a great number of teachers to say what
> their itching ears want to hear. (2 Timothy 4:3)

Brothers and sisters, we are living in that time. The lies are so thick that there is confusion everywhere, even in the Church. The "powerful delusion" is having its diabolical effect. Up is down. Left is right. Right is wrong. And boys are girls. It is madness.

But Jesus.

Those two words bring us hope. When we are confused and unsure which direction to turn, Jesus is steady as—well, steady as the Son of God walking on the water despite the wind and the waves. He will not let us down. He will not shift with culture. He refuses to bend.

> Therefore everyone who hears these words of mine and puts
> them into practice is like a wise man who built his house
> on the rock. The rain came down, the streams rose, and
> the winds blew and beat against that house; yet it did not
> fall, because it had its foundation on the rock. But everyone
> who hears these words of mine and does not put them into
> practice is like a foolish man who built his house on sand.
> The rain came down, the streams rose, and the winds blew
> and beat against that house, and it fell with a great crash.
> (Matthew 7:24–27)

Jesus has warned us not to take His words for granted. They're not optional. They are the rule of life. We cannot afford to bend to the culture if it pulls us even one hair further away from Jesus. What's more—He actually demands the culture bend to Him:

> Why do the nations conspire and the peoples plot in
> vain? The kings of the earth rise up and the rulers band

together against the Lord and against his anointed, saying, "Let us break their chains and throw off their shackles." (Psalm 2:1–3)

In case you haven't been paying attention, this is where we are right now. The nations, the culture, and the elite among us—they're all raging against the Lord. And many who claim the name of Christ are joining in through their affirmation of sin and celebration of that which breaks Heaven's heart. But God is not mocked. He will have the final say:

Kiss his Son, or he will be angry and your way will lead to your destruction, for his wrath can flare up in a moment. Blessed are all who take refuge in him. (Psalm 2:12)

Friend, I hope you have chosen to take refuge in Him. As the powerful delusion continues to spread, we need men and women who love the Lord to stand firmly for truth, to push back against the lies, and to be willing to suffer for the truth if need be. I am reminded of the story of Shadrach, Meshach, and Abednego. These three exiles from Judah were serving in Nebuchadnezzar's court when there came a powerful delusion like most have never seen.

King Nebuchadnezzar made an image of gold, sixty cubits high and six cubits wide, and set it up on the plain of Dura in the province of Babylon. He then summoned the satraps, prefects, governors, advisers, treasurers, judges, magistrates and all the other provincial officials to come to the dedication of the image he had set up. So the satraps, prefects, governors, advisers, treasurers, judges, magistrates and all the other provincial officials assembled for the dedication of the image that King Nebuchadnezzar had set up, and they stood before it.

Then the herald loudly proclaimed, "Nations and peoples of every language, this is what you are commanded to do: As soon as you hear the sound of the horn, flute, zither, lyre, harp, pipe and all kinds of music, you must fall down and worship the image of gold that King Nebuchadnezzar has set up. Whoever does not fall down and worship will immediately be thrown into a blazing furnace."

Therefore, as soon as they heard the sound of the horn, flute, zither, lyre, harp and all kinds of music, all the nations and peoples of every language fell down and worshiped the image of gold that King Nebuchadnezzar had set up. (Daniel 3:1–7)

Just imagine that. One minute, everything is normal. People throughout the Babylonian Empire are going about their business, taking care of their families, doing the everyday stuff of life. Then, Nebuchadnezzar sets up a golden image and declares that when the music starts pumping, everyone has to bow down and worship it. No one questions it. No one pushes back. This hunk of gold was just shiny metal, and now it's worthy of everyone's undying affection. That is a strong delusion.

But just think about what happened here. One minute, boys were boys and girls were girls; marriage was the sacred union between one man and one woman; and no one had to say "black lives matter" because—duh! But then, as if overnight, the whole nation is pledging their allegiance to the equality flag and declaring proper grammar is racist. And the Left didn't even need music to get everyone to bow down.

Shadrach, Meshach, and Abednego saw through the confusion of their day, though. They saw through the lies and the fear, and they recognized that golden idol was just a shiny hunk of metal that deserved none of their worship. The God of Israel alone was to be worshiped, and they refused to use Nebuchadnezzar's preferred pronouns—er, worship his blasphemous golden image. I love what they say when they are faced with losing everything, including their lives:

> Shadrach, Meshach and Abednego replied to him, "King Nebuchadnezzar, we do not need to defend ourselves before you in this matter. If we are thrown into the blazing furnace, the God we serve is able to deliver us from it, and he will deliver us from Your Majesty's hand. But even if he does not, we want you to know, Your Majesty, that we will not serve your gods or worship the image of gold you have set up." (Daniel 3:16–18)

In other words, Shadrach, Meshach, and Abednego told the king, "No matter what you do to us, we will not say this grand lie of yours is true. It doesn't matter who you are or what you do to us. Instead, we will stand on the truth, until the Truth Himself sets us free or He takes us home!"

That right there is the kind of civil disobedience we need. Unbending. Unyielding. Unflinching.

The days are dark. There's no doubt about that. Even so, that is no excuse not to stand. In fact, that's all the more reason. There may never be a better time to stand firm and show the powers of this world and the forces of evil that you cannot be hoodwinked.

ENDNOTES

Introduction: The Lies That Make Us

1   Wendell Husebø, "Report: NYT Twice Changes Reckless Headline: 'Israeli Strike Kills Hundreds in Hospital, Palestinians Say,'" Breitbart, October 18, 2023, https://www.breitbart.com/politics/2023/10/18/report-nyt-twice-changes-reckless-headline-israeli-strike-kills-hundreds-hospital-palestinians-say.

2   David Zweig, "NYT Uses Photo of Wrong Location for Hospital Story," Silent Lunch (Substack), October 18, 2023, https://www.silentlunch.net/p/nyt-uses-photo-of-wrong-location.

3   Matthew Phelan, "Hundreds of UFOs Have Been Spotted 'All Over the World,' Pentagon Chief Admits as NASA Unveils Findings into First Ever Study of Unexplained Phenomena in the Skies," Daily Mail, May 31, 2023, https://www.dailymail.co.uk/sciencetech/article-12144193/NASAs-UFO-task-force-livestream-historic-public-meeting-TODAY-Watch-here.html.

Chapter 1: Lie #1: America Is a Racist Nation

1   MSNBC, "'Widespread Agreement' in NBC Poll That American Society Is Racist," YouTube, April 27, 2023, https://www.youtube.com/watch?v=VqFQ7oPDkLs&t=108s.

2   "Ahmaud Arbery: What You Need to Know About the Case," BBC News, November 22, 2021, https://www.bbc.com/news/world-us-canada-52623151.

3   Juliana Menasce Horowitz, Anna Brown, and Kiana Cox, "Race in America in 2019," Pew Research Center, April 9, 2019, https://www. pewresearch.org/social-trends/2019/04/09/race-in-america-2019.

4   Ibid.

5   Christine Tamir and Monica Anderson, "One-in-Ten Black People Living in the U.S. Are Immigrants," Pew Research Center, January 20, 2022, https://www.pewresearch.org/race-ethnicity/2022/01/20/one-in-ten-black-people-living-in-the-u-s-are-immigrants.

6   "Income and Wealth in the United States: An Overview of Data," Peter G. Peterson Foundation, November 9, 2023, https://www.pgpf.org/blog/2023/02/income-and-wealth-in-the-united-states-an-overview-of-recent-data.

7   Yohuru Williams, "Why Thomas Jefferson's Anti-Slavery Passage Was Removed from the Declaration of Independence," History, updated June 26, 2023, https://www.history.com/news/declaration-of-independence-deleted-anti-slavery-clause-jefferson.

8   Abraham Lincoln, "Speech at Lewiston, Illinois," August 17, 1858, Abraham Lincoln Online, accessed July 16, 2023, https://www.abrahamlincolnonline.org/lincoln/speeches/faithquotes.htm.

9   "Civil War Casualties," HistoryNet, accessed July 16, 2023, https://www.historynet.com/civil-war-casualties.

10 "Civil War Casualties," American Battlefield Trust, updated September 15, 2023, https://www.battlefields.org/learn/articles/civil-war-casualties.

11 "On Views of Race and Inequality, Blacks and Whites Are Worlds Apart," Pew Research Center, June 27, 2016, https://www.pewresearch.org/social-trends/2016/06/27/1-demographic-\trends-and-economic-well-being.

12 Cherrie Bucknor, "Young Black America Part Two: College Entry and Completion," Center for Economic and Policy

Research, Issue Brief April 2015, https://cepr.net/documents
/black-college-entry-grad-rates-2015-04.pdf.

13 Brian Bridges, "African Americans and College Education by
the Numbers," United Negro College Fund, accessed July 17,
2023, https://uncf.org/the-latest/african-americans-and-college
-education-by-the-numbers.

14 Jeremy Horpedahl, "The Growth of Black Families Income,"
Economist Writing Every Day, February 8, 2023, https
://economistwritingeveryday.com/2023/02/08/the-growth-of
-black-families-income.

15 Dennis Prager, "5 Arguments against 'America Is a Racist
Country,'" RealClearPolitics, July 14, 2020, https://www
.realclearpolitics.com/articles/2020/07/14/5_arguments
_against_america_is_a_racist_country_143702.html#!.

16 Sam Charles, "After 3 Years of Progress, Chicago's Murder
Tally Skyrockets in 2020," *Chicago Sun Times*, December 31,
2020, https://chicago.suntimes.com/crime/2020/12/31/22208002
/chicago-murders-2020-skyrocket-crime-violence-cpd
-homicides.

17 Bradley Devlin, "95% of Murder Victims in Chicago This Year
Are People of Color," Daily Caller, September 17, 2020, https
://dailycaller.com/2020/09/17/murder-victims-minorities
-people-of-color-chicago-2020-homicide-operation-legend.

18 Matt Rosenberg and Ted Dabrowski, "Unwed Births, Illiterate
Children, and Black-on-Black Crime: What Chicago's Mayoral
Candidates Ignore," Wirepoints, February 14, 2023, https
://wirepoints.org/unwed-births-illiterate-children-and-black
-on-black-crime-what-chicagos-mayoral-candidates-ignore
-wirepoints.

19 "42d. Booker T. Washington," U.S. History, accessed October
19, 2023, https://www.ushistory.org/us/42d.asp.

Chapter 2: Lie #2: Being Pro-Life Is Only for White Evangelicals

1 "Abortion Rises in Importance as a Voting Issue, Driven by Democrats," Pew Research Center, August 23, 2022, https://www.pewresearch.org/politics/2022/08/23/abortion-rises-in-importance-as-a-voting-issue-driven-by-democrats/pp_2022-08-23_midterms_01-01.

2 Frank Newport, "Black Americans and Abortion," Gallup, September 3, 2020, https://news.gallup.com/opinion/polling-matters/318932/black-americans-abortion.aspx.

3 Ibid. These data are based on aggregated samples of interviews conducted as part of Gallup's May "Values and Beliefs" polls from 2001 to 2007 and from 2017 to 2020.

4 The first black House member, Joseph Rainey, began serving in 1870; the Democrats didn't elect a black person to the House for another sixty-five years!

5 Karen Grigsby Bates, "Why Did Black Voters Flee the Republican Party in the 1960s?" *Morning Edition*, July 14, 2014, https://www.npr.org/sections/codeswitch/2014/07/14/331298996/why-did-black-voters-flee-the-republican-party-in-the-1960s.

6 The quotation first appeared in print in Ronald Kessler's 1995 book *Inside the White House*. While some today doubt its authenticity, many believe the statement to be true, as LBJ was known to use the N-word with abandon; see Adam Serwer, "Lyndon Johnson Was a Civil Rights Hero. But He Was Also a Racist," MSNBC, April 11, 2014, https://www.msnbc.com/msnbc/lyndon-johnson-civil-rights-racism-msna305591.

7 Christina Bennett, "Abortion's Impact on the Black Community," Focus on the Family, December 7, 2021, https://www.focusonthefamily.com/pro-life/discovering-abortions-impact-on-the-black-community-moved-me-from-apathy-to-action.

8   Carole Novielli, "Reverend Jesse Jackson's Abortion Flip Flop Timeline," Scribd, accessed August 12, 2023, http s://www.scribd.com/document/172542300/Rev-Jesse-Jackson-s -abortion-flip-flop-timeline#.

9   Colman McCarthy, "Jackson's Reversal on Abortion," *Washington Post*, May 21, 1988, https://www.washingtonpost .com/archive/opinions/1988/05/21/jacksons-reversal-on -abortion/dd9e1637-020d-447b-9329-95ec67e41fd5.

10 Ibid.

11 Novielli, "Reverend Jesse Jackson's Abortion Flip Flop Timeline."

12 McCarthy, "Jackson's Reversal on Abortion."

13 Ibid.

14 Eric Bradner, Sarah Mucha, and Arlette Saenz, "Biden: 'If You Have a Problem Figuring Out Whether You're for Me or Trump, Then You Ain't Black'," CNN Politics, updated May 22, 2020, https://www.cnn.com/2020/05/22/politics/biden -charlamagne-tha-god-you-aint-black/index.html.

15 2010 Census results reveal that Planned Parenthood is targeting minority neighborhoods; 79 percent of its surgical abortion facilities are located within walking distance of black or Hispanic/Latino neighborhoods. "Planned Parenthood Targets Minority Neighborhoods," Protecting Black Life, https://www.protectingblacklife.org/pp_targets/index.html.

Chapter 3: Lie #3: Capitalism Is to Blame for Poverty

1   Rainer Zitelmann, "Is Capitalism to Blame for Hunger and Poverty?" Adam Smith Institute, June 24, 2021, https://www .adamsmith.org/blog/is-capitalism-to-blame-for-hunger-and -poverty.

2   Ibid.

3   Ibid. In this instance, an international dollar is a hypothetical
    unit of currency based on the worth of a single U.S. dollar
    in 1990.

4   Roger van Zwanenberg, "#84: Chinese Economic Growth after
    Mao, Part 2," Wealth and Power, April 1, 2022, https://www
    .wealthandpower.org/part-5/84-chinese-economic-growth
    -after-mao-part-2#.

5   While the official poverty rate is based on pre-tax income,
    it's viewed by many economists as a poor indicator of true
    deprivation. That's because it doesn't take into account other
    resources families may receive or their actual purchasing
    power. As its name suggests, the consumption poverty rate
    measures how much people consume in an economy.

6   Bruce D. Meyer and James X. Sullivan, "Annual Report on US
    Consumption Poverty: 2018," American Enterprise Institute,
    October 18, 2019, https://www.aei.org/research-products
    /report/annual-report-on-us-consumption-poverty-2018.

7   Lee Edwards, "The Case for Capitalism," The Heritage
    Foundation, May 21, 2020, https://www.heritage.org/
    conservatism/commentary/the-case-capitalism.

8   But thanks to capitalism, Lunsford now earns about $40,000
    per day. See Shannon Thaler, "'Rich Men North of Richmond'
    Singer Oliver Anthony Earning $40K per Day after Turning
    Down $8M Record Deal," New York Post, August 23, 2023,
    https://nypost.com/2023/08/23/oliver-anthony-earning-40000
    -per-day-from-rich-men-north-of-richmond.

9   Leonard E. Read, "I, Pencil: My Family Tree as Told by
    Leonard E. Read," Foundation for Economic Education,
    accessed August 28, 2023, first published in The Freeman,
    December 1958, available at https://fee.org/resources/i-pencil.

10 The "Invisible Hand" is a concept first developed by
    philosopher Adam Smith. It describes the way diverse
    people work together in a free market to create products
    and bring them to market, all without any central planning.

It's as though an "invisible hand" were orchestrating everyone's efforts.

11 Read, "I, Pencil."

Chapter 4: Lie #4: Christianity Is a White Man's Religion

1 E. J. Dickson, "Racists Are Worried about the Historical Accuracy of Mermaids," *Rolling Stone*, September 14, 2022, https://www.rollingstone.com/culture/culture-news/black-little-mermaid-racist-outcry-twitter-1234591724.

2 Cameron Bonomolo, "The Little Mermaid Director Defends Halle Bailey's Color-Blind Casting: 'Let's Find the Best Ariel,'" Comicbook, May 17, 2023, https://comicbook.com/movies/news/disney-the-little-mermaid-halle-bailey-ariel-director-rob-marshall-defends-color-blind-casting.

3 Dickson, "Racists Are Worried about the Historical Accuracy of Mermaids."

4 Alex Gurley, "Halle Bailey Shared How She Honestly Felt about the World's Reaction to Her Role in 'The Little Mermaid,'" Buzzfeed, March 21, 2023, https://www.buzzfeed.com/alexgurley/halle-bailey-little-mermaid-racist-backlash.

5 Jessica Winarski, "The Little Mermaid's Original Story Is Really about Gay Love and Rejection," CBR, updated February 26, 2023, https://www.cbr.com/hans-christian-andersen-gay-allegory-little-mermaid-disney.

6 Kwame Brown Bust Life, "Kwame Brown React to Pastor John Amanchukwu Mechee X Speaks Says Kwame Brown Is Not an Activist!" YouTube, September 1, 2023, https://www.youtube.com/watch?v=95leGoUxoZs.

7 Monique Duson, "4 Reasons Why Black Liberation Theology Is Another Gospel," The Center for Biblical Equality, January 11, 2022, https://www.centerforbiblicalunity.com/post/4-reasons-why-black-liberation-theology-is-another-gospel.

8   James H. Cone, *A Black Theology of Liberation* (1970; repr. ed., Maryknoll, New York: Orbis Books, 1990), 63.

9   The chart has since been removed from the official website of the National Museum of African American History and Culture (nmaahc.si.edu), but it still can be found in this news article: "National African-American Museum Removes, Apologizes for 'Whiteness' Chart," *New Tri-State Defender*, July 25, 2020, https://tri-statedefender.com/national-african-american-museum-removes-apologizes-for-whiteness-chart/07/25/.

10 PRRI Staff, "The 2020 PRRI Census of American Religion," Public Religion Research Institute, July 8, 2021, https://www.prri.org/research/2020-census-of-american-religion.

11 "Quick Facts," United States Census Bureau, https://www.census.gov/quickfacts/fact/table/US/PST045222.

12 PRRI Staff, "The 2020 PRRI Census of American Religion."

13 "Quick Facts," United States Census Bureau."

14 In full disclosure, when we add Roman Catholics into the mix, the picture does get a bit hazier. Twelve percent of the U.S. population identify as white Catholic, while less than 2 percent, or roughly three million people, identify as black Catholics. (See PRRI Staff, "The 2020 PRRI Census of American Religion" and "Faith among Black Americans: A Brief Overview of Black Religious History in the U.S.," Pew Research Center, February 16, 2021, https://www.pewresearch.org/religion/2021/02/16/a-brief-overview-of-black-religious-history-in-the-u-s/.)

15 Ibid.

16 Kelly Van Gilder, "Billy Graham's Heart for All Humanity: 'Christ Belongs to All People,'" Billy Graham Evangelistic Association, July 10, 2020, https://billygraham.org/story/billy-grahams-heart-for-all-humanity-christ-belongs-to-all-people.

17 "Quakers and Slavery," The Borthwick Institute for Archives: University of York, accessed September 14, 2023, https://www

.york.ac.uk/borthwick/holdings/research-guides/race/quakers
-and-slavery.

18   Frederick Douglass, "What, to a Slave, Is the Fourth of July?"
     (July 5, 1852), Black Past, January 24, 2007, https://www
     .blackpast.org/african-american-history/speeches-african
     -american-history/1852-frederick-douglass-what-slave-fourth
     -july.

19   Marcus W. Jernegan, "Slavery and Conversion in the
     American Colonies," *American Historical Review* 21, no. 3 (April
     1916): 505, https://www.jstor.org/stable/1835009?seq=2.

20   The scope of this chapter does not allow us to unpack all
     that the Bible teaches about slavery. However, it is important
     to realize that the early Church was birthed into a world
     where slavery was widespread, and the Gospel went forth
     into that world, inviting both slaves and slave owners into
     the Kingdom. Take Onesimus and Philemon, for example.
     Onesimus was a runaway slave whom Paul sent back to his
     master, Philemon, knowing full well that, legally, Philemon
     could have Onesimus put to death for his desertion. Paul
     did not command Philemon to set Onesimus free, at least
     not legally. Instead, he instructed him to treat Onesimus as a
     brother. "Perhaps the reason he was separated from you for
     a little while was that you might have him back forever—no
     longer as a slave, but better than a slave, as a dear brother"
     (Philemon 15–16). The Kingdom of God cannot endure
     slavery for long, because we were born—and born again—to
     be brothers and sisters.

Chapter 5: Lie #5: Debt Can Be Canceled

1   Ashlie Hughes, "The Boozy History of 'There's No Such
     Thing as a Free Lunch'," VinePair, September 7, 2020, https
     ://vinepair.com/articles/history-no-free-lunch.

2   Annie Nova, "What Biden's Student Loan Forgiveness Plan
     Would Mean for Borrowers," CNBC, updated November 16,
     2020, https://www.cnbc.com/2020/11/14/what-bidens-student
     -loan-forgiveness-plan-means-for-borrowers.html.

3   Chamber of Commerce Team, "Student Loan Statistics,"
     Chamber of Commerce, accessed September 22, 2023, https
     ://www.chamberofcommerce.org/student-loan-statistics.

4   Ibid.

5   Ibid.

6   Michael T. Nietzel, "New Study: College Degree Carries Big
     Earnings Premium, but Other Factors Matter Too," *Forbes*,
     October 11, 2021, https://www.forbes.com/sites
     /michaeltnietzel/2021/10/11/new-study-college-degree
     -carries-big-earnings-premium-but-other-factors-matter
     -too/?sh=6aa7375635cd.

7   Hear Reagan's comment from August 12, 1986, here:
     01101010charles, "The Nine Most Terrifying Words," YouTube,
     August 6, 2011, https://www.youtube.com/watch?v
     =xhYJS80MgYA.

8   "Tenth Amendment," Constitution Annotated, accessed
     September 24, 2023, https://constitution.congress.gov
     /constitution/amendment-10.

9   For a timeline of the federal student aid program, see Jeff
     Gitlen, "A Look into the History of Student Loans," LendEDU,
     May 2, 2023, https://lendedu.com/blog/history-of-student
     -loans.

10   William J. Bennett, "Our Greedy Colleges," *New York Times*,
     February 18, 1987, https://www.nytimes.com/1987/02/18
     /opinion/our-greedy-colleges.html.

11   A similar phenomenon takes place in the housing market
     with low-interest, thirty-year fixed mortgages. People are able
     to afford a monthly payment, so the overall price tag on the
     house matters little. Banks are willing to lend more because
     housing prices continue to rise, and since interest on a
     traditional mortgage is front-loaded, they make most of their

money in the first several years of a mortgage. The glut of cash available to consumers drives prices higher and higher, only slowing when the economy enters a recession or interest rates spike. But even then, there is rarely a downturn in housing prices—and when there is, it usually doesn't last long.

12   Erik Sherman, "College Tuition Is Rising at Twice the Inflation Rate—While Students Learn at Home," *Forbes*, August 31, 2020, https://www.forbes.com/sites /zengernews/2020/08/31/college-tuition-is-rising-at-twice -the-inflation-rate-while-students-learn-at-home/?sh =121a936e2f98.

13   David O. Lucca, Taylor Nadauld, and Karen Shen, "Credit Supply and the Rise in College Tuition: Evidence from the Expansion in Federal Student Aid Programs," *Review of Financial Studies*, 32, no. 2, February 2019, 423–66, https://doi .org/10.1093/rfs/hhy069.

14   In this discussion of biblical principles surrounding debt, we have not discussed the Jubilee Year, in which all debts were to be canceled and property was to be returned to its original owner (see Leviticus 25). Some have cited this Jubilee Year as an example of debt being canceled. However, there are three points to consider: 1) there's actually no evidence that Israel ever actually practiced the Jubilee; 2) Jubilee would have applied to the whole society, and so its application wouldn't have benefited one group over another; and 3) because Jubilee was to be a planned and repeated event, agreements and pricing would have reflected the cancellation of debt and the return of property; land purchases would have essentially been long-term leases.

15   Lawrence Hurley, "Supreme Court Kills Biden Student Loan Relief Plan," NBC News, June 30, 2023, https://www.nbcnews .com/politics/supreme-court/supreme-court-rule-bidens -student-loan-forgiveness-plan-friday-rcna76874.

16   Ibid.

Chapter 6: Lie #6: Disagreement Means We Can No Longer Talk

1   Brackets original. Jay Cost, "James Madison's Lesson on Free Speech," *National Review,* September 4, 2017, https://www.nationalreview.com/2017/09/james-madison-free-speech-rights-must-be-absolute-nearly.

2   "2021 College Free Speech Rankings," College Pulse and RealClearEducation, September 23, 2021, https://reports.collegepulse.com/college-free-speech-rankings-2021.

3   David Bromell, "Words Are Not Weapons and Disagreement Is Not Hate," Stuff, March 23, 2023, https://www.stuff.co.nz/opinion/131568621/words-are-not-weapons-and-disagreement-is-not-hate.

4   Ibid.

5   Logan Albright, "Why We Should Resist Branding Others 'Hateful' Just Because We Disagree," FEE Stories, February 29, 2020, https://fee.org/articles/why-we-should-resist-branding-others-hateful-just-because-we-disagree.

6   Natalie O'Neill, "Inside Ruth Bader Ginsburg and Antonin Scalia's Unlikely Friendship," *New York Post*, September 23, 2020, https://nypost.com/article/inside-ruth-bader-ginsburg-and-antonin-scalias-friendship.

7   Pete Williams and Elisha Fieldstadt, "Justice Ruth Bader Ginsburg on Justice Antonin Scalia: 'We Were Best Buddies,'" NBC News, February 14, 2016, https://www.nbcnews.com/news/us-news/justice-ruth-bader-ginsburg-justice-antonin-scalia-we-were-best-n518671.

8   "Statements from the Supreme Court Regarding the Death of Antonin Scalia (Updated)," news release, Supreme Court of the United States, February 15, 2016, https://www.supremecourt.gov/publicinfo/press/pressreleases/pr_02-14-16.

9   "Cornel West & Robert George," *Firing Line with Martha Hoover*, PBS, November 26, 2021, https://www.pbs.org/wnet/firing-line/video/cornel-west-robert-george-lgrgwb.

10 Ibid.

11 Ibid.

12 James Dean, "West, George Defend Academic Freedom in Coors Forum," *Cornell Chronicle,* September 14, 2021, https://news.cornell.edu/stories/2021/09/west-george-defend -academic-freedom-coors-forum.

13 Timothy Friberg, Barbara Friberg, and Neva F. Miller, *Analytical Lexicon of the Greek New Testament*, Baker's Greek New Testament Library (Grand Rapids, Michigan: Baker Books, 2000), 158.

Chapter 7: Lie #7: Transgender People Are Under Attack

1 Simran Agarwal, "'Hate Has Consequences': Outrage as Trans Group Calls Nashville School Shooter Audrey Hale 'Victim of Hate' and Mourns His 'Tragic' Death," Meaww.com, updated March 28, 2023, https://meaww.com/outrage-as-trans -group-calls-shooter-audrey-hale-victim-of-hate-and-mourns -his-tragic-death; Andy Ngô (MrAndyNgo), "'Hate has consequences....,'" Twitter, 10:05 a.m., March 28, 2023, https://twitter.com/MrAndyNgo/status/1640746882640011264 ?ref_src=twsrc%5Etfw%7Ctwcamp%5Etweetembed%7Ctwterm %5E1640746882640011264%7Ctwgr%5Ee8798f8fbee2afbb5a27 453e591530d56cc935c9%7Ctwcon%5Es1_&ref_url=https%3A %2F%2Fmeaww.com%2Foutrage-as-trans-group-calls -shooter-audrey-hale-victim-of-hate-and-mourns-his-tragic -death.

2 Ngô, "Hate has consequences."

3 Ibid.

4 Laurel Duggan, "Media Twists Itself into Knots Covering Transgender School Shooter," The Daily Caller, March 28, 2023, https://dailycaller.com/2023/03/28/media-transgender -school-shooter-pronouns-audrey-hale.

5   Emily Schmall, "Most Mass Shooting Suspects Are Male," *New York Times,* updated April 13, 2023, https://www .nytimes.com/2023/03/27/us/woman-shooter-nashville .html?smtyp=cur&smid=tw-nytimes.

6   James Reinl, "'I Want the Manifesto'—Experts Explain Why You May Never Get to Read Nashville Shooter Audrey Hale's Screed, and Why It May Not Be the Blueprint for Transgender Terrorism That Many Expect," *Daily Mail*, April 5, 2023, https://www.dailymail.co.uk/news/article-11942059/Why -never-read-transgender-Nashville-shooter-Audrey-Hales -murderous-manifesto.html.

7   Matthew Impelli, "Audrey Hale's Manifesto Details Monthslong Plan to Commit Shooting," *Newsweek*, April 3, 2023, https://www.newsweek.com/audrey-hales-manifesto -details-monthslong-plan-commit-shooting-1792317.

8   Stephanie Pagones, "Parents' Efforts to Suppress Nashville School Shooter Audrey Hale's Manifesto Would Be Unprecedented If Granted: Expert," *New York Post*, July 28, 2023, https://nypost.com/2023/07/28/audrey-hale-manifesto -suppression-could-be-unprecedented.

9   No one can change their gender. That was given to them by God and it is encoded in their DNA. No matter how many puberty blockers or surgeries a person undergoes, the most they will do is change their appearance and mutilate the body they have been given. Language is important. In truth, we should not even use terms like "transgender" or "gender dysphoria," because they are loaded with meaning that opposes the truth of nature and nature's God. But in order to make this chapter understandable, I have been somewhat forced to use the language of our culture as it currently exists.

10 Jeff Myers and Brandon Showalter, *Exposing the Gender Lie: How to Protect Children and Teens from the Transgender Industry's False Ideology* (Manitou Springs, Colorado: Summit Ministries, in association with *The Christian Post*, 2023), 64;

https://summitfiles.org/content/general/Exposing-the
-Gender-Lie_SM-CP_2023.pdf.

11 Ibid., 12.

12 Kim Parker, Juliana Menasce Horowitz, and Anna Brown,
"Americans' Complex Views on Gender Identity and
Transgender Issues," Pew Research Center, June 28, 2022,
https://www.pewresearch.org/social-trends/2022/06/28
/americans-complex-views-on-gender-identity-and
-transgender-issues.

13 Riittakerttu Kaltiala, "'Gender-Affirming Care Is Dangerous.
I Know Because I Helped Pioneer It.'," The Free Press,
October 30, 2023, https://www.thefp.com/p/gender-affirming
-care-dangerous-finland-doctor.

14 Ibid.

15 Ibid.

16 Aidan Hulting, "Former D20 Student Accused of Planning
Attacks on Three Campuses," KOAA News 5 Southern
Colorado, April 7, 2023, https://www.koaa.com/news/covering
-colorado/former-d20-student-accused-of-planning-attacks
-on-three-campuses.

17 Christopher Tremoglie, "Trans Children Aren't under Attack,
but Christian Children Are," *Washington Examiner*, April 7,
2023, https://www.washingtonexaminer.com/opinion/trans
-children-arent-under-attack-but-christian-children-are.

18 Drew Wilder, Gina Cook, and The Associated Press, "Family
of Loudoun Co. Student Sexually Assaulted: 'Ineptitude of
All Involved Is Staggering'," NBC 4 Washington, December 12,
2022, https://www.nbcwashington.com/news/local/family
-of-loudoun-co-student-sexually-assaulted-ineptitude-of-all
-involved-is-staggering/3231725.

19 Kendall Tietz, "Judge Finds Skirt-Wearing Teen Boy Guilty of
Sexually Assaulting Female Classmate in Loudoun County
School Bathroom," Daily Caller, October 26, 2021, https
://dailycaller.com/2021/10/26/skirt-teen-loudon-county-public
-schools-sexual-assault-guilty.

20 Kate Davison and 7News Staff, "Loudoun Co. Former Superintendent Ziegler, School Official Indicted by Special Grand Jury," ABC 7News, December 12, 2022, https://wjla .com/news/local/loudoun-county-schools-indictments-grand -jury-charges-scott-ziegler-wayde-byard-pio-superintendent -virginia-attorney-general-jason-miyares-lcps-sex-assaults -report-cases-fired-interim-emergency-meeting-va-education.

21 Susan Ciancio, "Gender Dysphoria in the DSM-5: The Change in Terminology," Human Life International, February 25, 2022, https://www.hli.org/resources/dsm-5-gender -dysphoria.

22 Ross Toro, "How Gender Reassignment Surgery Works (Infographic)," Live Science, August 26, 2013, https://www .livescience.com/39170-how-gender-reassignment-surgery -works-infographic.html.

23 Ibid.

24 Katie Couric and Kaye Foley, "The North Carolina 'Bathroom Bill' HB2 Explained," Yahoo! News, April 1, 2016, https ://news.yahoo.com/the-north-carolina-bathroom-bill-hb2 -explained-172020141.html.

25 HB2 was signed into law on March 23, 2016, by Governor Pat McCrory, but the provision concerning public facilities—the heart of the bill—was repealed a year later with the passage of HB 142 on March 30, 2017. See Corinne Segal, "What the North Carolina Legislation to Repeal the HB2 'Bathroom Bill' Actually Says," *PBS News Hour*, March 30, 2017, https://www .pbs.org/newshour/nation/watch-live-nc-legislature-debates -repeal-hb2-bathroom-bill.

26 Lisa Littman, "Parent Reports of Adolescents and Young Adults Perceived to Show Signs of a Rapid Onset of Gender Dysphoria," *PLOS One* 13, no. 8 (August 2018): e0202330, https://doi.org/10.1371/journal.pone.0202330.

27 Is it any wonder, then, that parents are rightly concerned about the LGBTQ+ agenda infiltrating children's television shows? For instance, in a *Paw Patrol* spinoff called *Rubble & Crew*, writers introduced the first nonbinary character. "Screenwriter and activist Lindz Amer called helping develop the character 'a bucket list item.'" See John Russell, "'Paw Patrol' Franchise Introduces Its First Non-Binary Character," LGBTQNation, September 21, 2023, https://www.lgbtqnation .com/2023/09/paw-patrol-franchise-introduces-its-first-non -binary-character. There is no reason for talking dogs to be discussing their sexual preferences or gender identities; there can be no other rationale for such nonsense other than the grooming of small children. The *Paw Patrol* universe is not the only kids' property to see such introductions. *The Transformers* also introduced a nonbinary character. See Alyssa Mercante, "New *Transformers* Series Introduces Its First Nonbinary Robot [Update]," Kotaku, November 14, 2022, https://kotaku .com/transformers-earthspark-nightshade-nonbinary-robot -lgbt-1849781910. These two join other well-known shows in introducing children to LGBTQ+ propaganda, including *Rugrats, Doc McStuffins,* and the world of *Toy Story* through the film *Lightyear*. See Josie Powell, "16 Kids Shows with LGBTQIA+ Characters and Storylines," Care., June 9, 2023, https://www.care.com/c/kids-shows-with-lgbtq-characters -and-storylines.

28 Alyssa Jackson, "The High Cost of Being Transgender," CNN, July 31, 2015, https://www.cnn.com/2015/07/31/health /transgender-costs-irpt/index.html.

29 "Hearing on Gender-Affirming Care for Minors," C-SPAN, July 27, 2023, https://www.c-span.org/video/?529599-1/hearing -gender-affirming-care-minors.

30 This is by design. Satan knows what he's doing in his attempts to keep people in bondage.

Chapter 8: Lie #8: If You're against Pornography, You're a Book-Banner

1   Robie H. Harris and Michael Emberley, *It's Perfectly Normal: Changing Bodies, Growing Up, Sex, Gender, and Sexual Health* (Somerville, Massachusetts: Candlewick Press, 2014), 56.

2   Ibid.

3   Alexi Giannoulias, "First-in-the-Nation Legislation to Prevent Book Bans Approved by General Assembly," Illinois Secretary of State, May 3, 2023, https://www.ilsos.gov/news/2023/may/230503d1.pdf.

4   Forbes Breaking News, "SHOCKING MOMENT: John Kennedy Reads Graphic Quotes from Children's Books at Senate Hearing," YouTube, September 12, 2023, https://www.youtube.com/watch?v=KBhy_vlgKS4.

5   Ibid.

6   Brendan O'Brien, "Illinois Becomes First State to Pass Law Curtailing Book Bans," Reuters, June 13, 2023, https://www.reuters.com/world/us/illinois-becomes-first-state-pass-law-curtailing-book-bans-2023-06-13.

7   "SHOCKING MOMENT: John Kennedy Reads Graphic Quotes from Children's Books at Senate Hearing."

8   Bonchie, "Democrats Froth and Seethe after John Kennedy Reads 'Gender Queer' during Senate Hearing," RedState, September 12, 2023, https://redstate.com/bonchie/2023/09/12/watch-sen-kennedy-leaves-liberals-seething-after-he-reads-gender-queer-during-a-hearing-n2163722.

9   Mary Yang, "'Authoritarian Regimes Ban Books': Democrats Raise Alarm at Senate Hearing," *The Guardian*, September 12, 2023, https://www.theguardian.com/us-news/2023/sep/12/senate-book-bans-hearing-lgbtq.

10 Ellipses original. Brooke Stephens, "Protecting Kids from Explicit Material Shouldn't Be Controversial," Public Square

Magazine, October 10, 2022, https://publicsquaremag.org
/sexuality-family/parenting/protecting-kids-from-explicit
-material-shouldnt-be-controversial, citing "Voters against
Obscene Books in Public Schools," Rasmussen Reports,
October 3, 2022, https://www.rasmussenreports.com
/public_content/politics/partner_surveys/voters_against
_obscene_books_in_public_schools and Marjorie Cortez,
"American Family Survey: Are Public Schools the Battlefield
for the Nation's Culture Wars?" *Deseret News*, October 4, 2022,
https://www.deseret.com/2022/10/4/23363910/public-schools
-battlefield-nation-culture-wars-book-bans-lgbtq-trans
-american-family-survey.

11 Ibid.

12 Valerie Peterson, "Young Adult and New Adult Book
Markets," liveaboutdotcom, December 15, 2018, https://www
.liveabout.com/the-young-adult-book-market-2799954.

13 Jay Asher, *Thirteen Reasons Why* (New York: Razorbill,
2011), 265.

14 Mike Curato, *Flamer* (New York: Henry Holt & Co.: 2020), 14.

15 Ibid., 22.

16 Ibid., 23.

17 Ibid., 132.

18 Footage of this incident can be found here: John
Amanchukwu, "John Amanchukwu Is Kicked out of School
Board Meeting by Sheriffs for Reading a Pornographic Book,"
YouTube, August 29, 2023, https://www.youtube.com
/watch?v=xS7HfezKfIQ.

19 Footage of this incident can be found here: TPUSA Faith,
"THROWN OUT OF A SCHOOL BOARD MEETING IN
NEVADA Ft. John Amanchukwu | TPUSA Faith," YouTube,
October 2, 2023, https://www.youtube.com/watch?v=9
_D-ivIJRyU.

Chapter 9: Lie #9: The Bible Isn't Political, So Christians Should Stay Out of Politics

1   "Black-Robed Regiment," National History Education Clearinghouse, accessed October 12, 2023, https://teachinghistory.org/history-content/ask-a-historian/24635.

2   Craig Greenfield, "Yes, the Bible Talks about Politics All the Time," craiggreenfield.com, January 23, 2019, https://www.craiggreenfield.com/blog/jesuspolitics.

3   Bibelhaus ErlebnisMuseum editors, "Calendar Inscription from Priene," Bibelhaus ErlebnisMuseum, accessed October 15, 2023, https://www.bibelhaus-frankfurt.de/en/bimumag/the-special-object/calendar-inscription-from-priene.

4   Frederick William Danker, ed., *A Greek-English Lexicon of the New Testament and Other Early Christian Literature*, 3rd ed. (Chicago: University of Chicago Press, 2000), 303.

5   Wayne Grudem, *Politics according to the Bible: A Comprehensive Resource for Understanding Modern Political Issues in Light of Scripture* (Grand Rapids, Michigan: Zondervan, 2010), 48.

6   Left-leaning media outlets have praised *Christianity Today* for punching right, pointing out hypocrisy in the Church, and generally providing cover for progressive agenda points. See, for example, Jacob Lupfer, "Why a 'Yes' to Gays Is Often a 'No' to Evangelicalism (COMMENTARY)," *The Washington Post*, June 10, 2015, https://www.washingtonpost.com/national/religion/why-a-yes-to-gays-is-often-a-no-to-evangelicalism-commentary/2015/06/10/d8657e06-0fa6-11e5-a0fe-dccfea4653ee_story.html.

7   Mark Galli, "Trump Should Be Removed from Office," *Christianity Today*, December 19, 2019, https://www.christianitytoday.com/ct/2019/december-web-only/trump-should-be-removed-from-office.html.

8   Megan Basham, "Christianity Today Staff Made Extensive Campaign Donations between 2015 and 2022 . . . All Went to Democrats," The Daily Wire, October 11, 2023, https

://www.dailywire.com/news/christianity-today-staff-made
-extensive-campaign-donations-between-2015-and-2022
-all-went-to-democrats. The specific search data from the
Federal Election Commission on which Basham's story is
based can be seen at https://www.fec.gov/data/receipts
/individual-contributions/?data_type=processed&contributor
_employer=christianity+today&contributor_employer
=christianity+today+international&two_year_transaction
_period=2014&two_year_transaction_period=2016&two
_year_transaction_period=2018&two_year_transaction
_period=2020&two_year_transaction_period=2022.

9   Ibid.

10 "Is Progressive Christianity Dangerous?" *Christian Chronicle,*
    October 1, 2018, https://christianchronicle.org/is-progressive
    -christianity-dangerous.

11 Lucas Miles, *The Christian Left: How Liberal Thought Has
    Hijacked the Church* (Savage, Minnesota: BroadStreet
    Publishing, 2021), 18–19.

12 This trope has been making the rounds in recent years, based
    on a superficial reading of the Christmas story in Matthew
    2. Joseph, Mary, and Jesus do indeed flee to Egypt to escape
    Herod's wrath. But they are not refugees in any modern sense.
    First, nation states as we have them today didn't exist back
    then. There was no official border barring them from entering
    Egypt. Second, both Egypt and Judea were part of the Roman
    Empire—so technically speaking, Jesus's family never left the
    country. Third, as far as we can tell, Joseph, Mary, and Jesus
    paid their own way, probably by using proceeds from the
    gold, frankincense, and myrrh the wise men brought them
    (Matthew 2:11). There was also a sizeable Jewish population
    in Egypt in the first century. Therefore, it's likely they joined
    their fellow Jews during their sojourn. All that to say, they
    weren't dependent on the state. Fourth, their time in Egypt
    was always intended to be temporary. Once Herod the Great
    died, the family returned to Israel.

Chapter 10: Lie #10: The Church Is Not Essential

1   Max Jordan, Nguemeni Tiako and Kelsey C. Priest, "Yes, Liquor Stores Are Essential Businesses," *Scientific American,* April 7, 2020, https://blogs.scientificamerican.com /observations/yes-liquor-stores-are-essential-businesses.

2   "2 Strip Clubs Can Stay Open and Set Own COVID Rules, California Judge Rules," CBS News, December 17, 2020, https://www.cbsnews.com/news/strip-clubs-exempt-covid -rules-judge-san-diego-california.

3   Frank Barry, "3 Things to Think About before Opening Your Church's Doors after COVID 19," Tithe.ly Blog, May 26, 2020, https://get.tithe.ly/blog/reopen-church.

4   Will Maule, "21.5% of Non-Christians Say Coronavirus Pandemic Has Led Them to Start Reading the Bible, Study Finds," FaithWire, April 2, 2020, https://www.faithwire.com /2020/04/02/21-5-of-non-christians-say-coronavirus-pandemic -has-led-them-to-start-reading-the-bible-study-finds.

5   Ellipsis original. Michael Gryboski, "Pastor John MacArthur Rejects Online Worship, Says Zoom Is 'Not Church,'" *The Christian Post,* November 11, 2021, https://www.christianpost .com/news/pastor-john-macarthur-rejects-online-worship-its -not-church.html.

6   "First Amendment," Constitution Annotated, accessed October 16, 2023, https://constitution.congress.gov /constitution/amendment-1.

7   Jesse T. Jackson, "California Judge Orders NO Indoor Worship Services for John MacArthur and Grace Community Church," ChurchLeaders, September 11, 2020, https://churchleaders .com/news/382126-california-judge-orders-no-indoor-worship -services-for-john-macarthur-and-grace-community-church. html.

8   Jaclyn Cosgrove, "Why L.A. County Paid $400,000 to a Church That Violated Coronavirus Rules," *Los Angeles Times,*

September 2, 2021, https://www.latimes.com/california
/story/2021-09-02/why-l-a-county-paid-400-000-to-a-church
-that-violated-coronavirus-rules.

9   Jeremiah Johnson, "Church Is Essential," Grace to You Blog,
July 12, 2021, https://www.gty.org/library/blog/B210712/church
-is-essential.

10   Cheryl Platzman Weinstock, "How Church May Boost Mental
Health," AARP, September 9, 2019, https://www.aarp.org/health
/healthy-living/info-2019/religion-and-mental-health.html.

11   Frank Newport, "Religion and Wellbeing in the U.S.: Update,"
Gallup, February 4, 2022, https://news.gallup.com/opinion
/polling-matters/389510/religion-wellbeing-update.aspx.

12   Paulina Napierała, "Black Churches and Their Attitudes
to the Social Protest in the Civil Rights Era: Obedience,
Civil Disobedience and Black Liberation Theology," *Studia
Migracyjne—Przegląd Polonijny* 2, no. 176 (2020): 259.

13   Ibid., 263.

14   Paul David Tripp, "5 Ways the COVID-19 Pandemic Points Us
to the Gospel," Crossway Blog, April 4, 2020, https://www
.crossway.org/articles/5-ways-the-covid-19-pandemic-points
-us-to-the-gospel.

15   Michael S. Heiser, "What Did Jesus Mean by "Gates of Hell"?
Word by Word, April 10, 2018, https://www.logos.com/grow
/jesus-mean-gates-hell.

Afterword: A Powerful Delusion, or a Short
Bible Study on the End Times

1   By "BLM," I'm referring to the Marxist organization Black
Lives Matter—an anti-Christian, anti-family militia for the
Democrat Party that is as racist as it is ungodly. I am not
referring to well-meaning people who repeat the phrase *black
lives matter*. Of course black lives matter.